William Harbutt Dawson

Social Switzerland

Studies of Present-day Social Movements and Legislation in the Swiss Republic

William Harbutt Dawson

Social Switzerland
Studies of Present-day Social Movements and Legislation in the Swiss Republic

ISBN/EAN: 9783744728041

Printed in Europe, USA, Canada, Australia, Japan

Cover: Foto ©Suzi / pixelio.de

More available books at **www.hansebooks.com**

Social Switzerland

Social Switzerland

STUDIES OF PRESENT-DAY SOCIAL MOVEMENTS AND
LEGISLATION IN THE SWISS REPUBLIC

BY

WILLIAM HARBUTT DAWSON

AUTHOR OF

"GERMANY AND THE GERMANS," "GERMAN SOCIALISM AND FERDINAND
LASSALLE," "PRINCE BISMARCK AND STATE SOCIALISM," ETC.

LONDON: CHAPMAN & HALL, Ld.

1897

RICHARD CLAY & SONS, LIMITED,
LONDON & BUNGAY.

TO

A. C. A. D.

PREFACE

I DO not think that this little book needs an apology. The investigations of which it is a record were undertaken in the hope and belief that the experience of Switzerland, in not a few directions of social reform, would prove of assistance in our own country, by throwing light, not indeed upon our problems—for these are clear and plain to view—but upon the treatment of them.

Those who have taken the trouble to observe and inquire must have been impressed by the boldness and originality which the Cantonal and Municipal Governments of the Swiss Republic have shown of late years in their manifold excursions in the field of social reform. For there, as here and everywhere, new social ideas and forces are at work, softening the human relationship in various ways—between rich and poor, between employer and employed, between the governing and the governed. I believe we may learn much from the ameliorative movements which are going on so near our own doors. The conditions may, to some extent, be different, but the problems themselves are the same.

Therefore I place this record of another people's doings in one of the most important departments of political and economic activity at the service of statesmen and social students at home, and of all who believe that the peace, happiness, and progress of society can best—nay alone—be attained by the way of organic reform, trusting that it will at least inform where it need not stimulate.

W. H. D.

CONTENTS

I

THE ORGANISATION

AND

PROTECTION OF LABOUR

B

CHAPTER I

THE FEDERAL FACTORY LAWS AND THE WORKING CLASSES

THE existing federal factory legislation of Switzerland substantially dates from March 23, 1877, and was adopted by virtue of a clause introduced into the federal constitution of 1874, giving to the Confederation the right to "enact uniform regulations upon the work of children in factories, upon the duration of the work of adults therein, and for the protection which should be accorded to workpeople employed in unhealthy and dangerous industries."

The due administration of the law is the duty of the Federal Government, the Cantonal Authorities, and the Factory Inspectors together. The last are three in number, and to them the country is divided out as follows into three circuits (Kreise):—First circuit, comprising the cantons of Zurich, Uri, Schwyz, Obwalden, Nidwalden, Glarus, Zug, St. Gall, and Grisons. Second—Berne (Jura), Freiburg, Ticino, Vaud, Valais, Neuchâtel, and Geneva. Third

3

—Berne (old portions), Lucerne, Soleure, Basle Urban and Rural, Schaffhausen, the Appenzells, Aargau, and Thurgau. For many years the Factory Inspectors have been Dr. F. Schuler for the first circuit, Herr H. Rauschenbach for the second, and M. Ami Campiche for the third.

The Inspectors, or their assistants, or both together, visit all the factories in their districts at least once a year, and many of them twice or thrice. They report that though the relationship with the employers is as a rule friendly, strange exceptions are not uncommon, proving that the Factory Act has not yet commended itself universally as a measure of necessity. Perhaps the oddest incident related in the last joint-report of the Inspectors is one which tells how a small manufacturer, incensed at the intrusion of the law's guardian, called his overseers round him, and in the presence of this official gave them strict command that he should never be allowed to enter the building again. The irate employer was, of course, proceeded against and duly warned. Nor are the functions of the Inspectors confined to factory visiting. Herr Rauschenbach states that working people appeal to them in increasing numbers for advice and help on subjects like employers' liability, wages deductions, disagreement concerning notice, sick insurance, irregularities in the factories, etc., and women do this almost as readily as men. Now and then, too, it happens that the interposition of the Inspector is able to prevent a threatened strike.

To come to the Factory Act itself. According to its original terms the Act applies to all industrial establishments in which "a more or less considerable number of workpeople" are "occupied simultaneously and regularly out of their dwellings, and in a closed building." Such buildings were to be constituted factories for the purposes of the Act, and when there was uncertainty as to the application of the covering clause the Federal Government was (and now has) to determine the matter without reference to the Government of the canton in which the concern affected was situated. The obscurity of the definition of "a factory" soon led to difficulty, and it was found necessary to resort to a more obvious description. In accordance with a resolution of the Government, of June 3, 1891, the word is now accepted as indicating any industrial establishment employing more than five persons, or employing persons under eighteen years of age, and working with machine power, or offering peculiar dangers to the health and life of the workpeople; otherwise, the requisite number of employees to constitute a concern or factory is eleven and upwards. In June, 1895, the number of factories amenable to the federal law was 4933; it now exceeds 5000.

The essential provisions of the Act are the following. It is required that all work-rooms and machinery shall be kept in such a state as shall not be injurious to the life or health of the workpeople. The light and ventilation must be ample, all dangerous parts of machinery must be carefully guarded, and in general all the measures be taken which science and invention suggest for the lessening of risk and injury. When an accident occurs, whether fatal or not, the employer must at once report it to the local authority competent in the matter, which will institute an inquiry into the whole circumstances, and inform the Cantonal Government of the facts. The legal liability of the factory owner in regard to accidents extends to all injuries sustained by employees which have been caused to the latter in the discharge of their duties, or by the default of the managers, overseers, or other representative officials, unless it can be proved that the accident was due to unpreventable causes (*force majeure*) or to negligence on the part of the victim. In the latter event the employer does not necessarily escape scot-free, but the compensation awardable is proportionately reduced. All factory regulations—as to the conditions and hours of work, payment of wages, fines, etc.— must be submitted to the Cantonal Government, which first takes the opinion thereon of the workpeople. In this connection it is laid down that no fine may exceed half-a-day's wages, and the sums thus retained by an employer must be used for the benefit of the workpeople, and particularly in provision for sick relief. Deductions from wages for defective work or waste of raw material do not, however, count as fines. In the absence of written agreement to the contrary, at least fourteen days' notice is necessary in the event of determining employment on either side, though it is often longer. It is specifically laid down that employers shall see to the due observance of "good manners and regard for the proprieties" in their work-rooms. Employers must in general pay their workpeople at least once a fortnight in legal tender, and on the factory premises.

The law fixes a normal day of eleven hours, though ten hours only may be worked on Saturday and the days preceding holidays; and this period must elapse between the hours of 5 a.m. and 8 p.m. in the months of June, July, and August, and 6 a.m. and 8 p.m. during the remainder of the year. In the case of injurious occupations, however, the Federal Council fixes the hours which may be worked. Overtime and night work (*i. e.* between 8 p.m. and 5 or 6 a.m. according to the season) may only be resorted to by permission, and in no case may a workman be required against his will to work beyond the normal hours. In the middle of the day at least an hour's rest must be given to all workpeople, and for the convenience of those who prefer to take their meals at the works suitable rooms must be provided. An exception from the normal work-

time is made in the case of industries in which
uninterrupted work is necessary, but here special
regulations are laid down by the Federal Council.
Here, too, Sunday work may be followed, but not in
other cases unless by express permission and under
exceptional circumstances. Where, however, Sunday
work is the rule, every employee must have alternate
Sundays free. The festivals are determined separately in each canton by the Government of the
same, but the number of such days may not exceed
eight in the year, and they can only be declared
obligatory for members of the religious confessions
which observe them. At the same time a workman
who refuses to work on a religious festival which is
not comprised in the statutory eight holidays cannot
be punished.

Women are afforded special protection by the law.
In their case, Sunday and night work is forbidden
under all circumstances. Also, when they have
household duties to perform they may leave work
half-an-hour before noon, unless the mid-day pause
be an hour and a half. The provisions affecting
women in childbirth are in themselves rigid, but
they are not rigidly enforced. It is laid down that
both before and after childbirth a "close time"—
extending in all to at least eight weeks—shall be
observed, during which they shall not be allowed to
work ; nor may they be re-admitted to the factory
without proof that six weeks have passed since their

confinement. Moreover, the Federal Council reserves the right to prohibit altogether the employment of pregnant women in certain branches of industry. As a matter of fact, these provisions are virtually a dead letter so far as relates to the period before confinement. Women so circumstanced generally insist on earning money as long as possible, and only when a slight payment is made to them during absence are they willing to stay away.

Children under the age of fourteen completed years may not legally be employed in factories, and in the case of those of between fifteen and sixteen years "the time reserved for educational and religious instruction may not be sacrificed to work in the factory." The form of expression observed here is significant. In regard to child labour, indeed, Switzerland continues to occupy a unique position. The federal delegate to the Berlin Labour Congress of 1890 strenuously endeavoured to string the rest of the States there represented up to the same year of fourteen, but in vain, and twelve years was declared by the Congress to be a fitting age at which to introduce a child to factory life, though even ten years in the case of Southern countries. Nevertheless, though the law is so decided and solicitous, cases are occasionally found in all the circuits of the employment of children under the protected age. A careful look-out is, however, kept by the Inspectors and their assistants, and the offenders are strictly dealt with.

Again, no "juveniles" under eighteen years may be employed at night or on Sunday, though in the case of industries requiring unintermittent work boys of from fourteen to eighteen may be so employed if it appears to be indispensable both to the work and to the technical training of the boys themselves, but here the Federal Council lays down special regulations as to the number of hours, and the health of the young workers.

Finally, any and every infringement of the law renders the transgressor liable to a fine of from 5 to 500 francs (4s. to £20), and in case of repeated offences to imprisonment up to three months.

A few instructive facts and figures may fittingly follow relative to the general conditions of work in the light of the statutory provisions above cited.

A thorough enumeration of the 4933 factories and workshops subject to the federal law which was instituted in June, 1895,[1] by the Department for

---

[1] The census card served upon each factory bore the following text:—

Canton............   District ....
Parish.............
Branch of industry............
No. of workpeople on June 5, 1895:
   14 to 18 years: male............   female...................
   18 to 50 „   „ ....   „ ....
   Over 50 „   „ ....   „ ....

Industry, established the fact that since the similar enumeration of 1888 the factory workers had increased 25·8 per cent.—from 159,543 to 200,199 (119,204 males and 80,995 females). The increase was not, however, either general or equal, the essentially industrial cantons showing a far larger increase than the rest. In Neuchâtel the increase was 122 per cent., in Geneva 74, and in Berne 50; while in St. Gall there had been a diminution of 4·5 per cent., and in Glarus one of 4·2, owing to the decay of the embroidery, calico-printing, and cotton-spinning industries. It is noticeable, however, that in general the census of the textile workers of Switzerland only showed an increase of 0·39 per cent. in the seven years. The industries which had increased most were the boot and shoe manufactures, with 75 per cent.; manufactures of food-stuffs and drinks, 30·9

Of these :
    Swiss................   *Austrians*................
    French...............   *English* ....
    Italians.............   *Other lands* ....
    Germans...........
No. of hours per week............
    Horse-power requisite for normal work............
Existing motive-power :
    Water........................   *horse*
    Gas..........................   *horse*
    Electricity....................   *horse*
    Steam ....   *horse*
    Petroleum, and the like......   *horse*
Firm..

per cent.; the chemical industry, 50·5 per cent.; paper-making and polygraphic industry, 50·4 per cent.; the metal industry, 139 per cent.; the machine industry, 45·1 per cent.; watch-making and jewellery industry, 31·6 per cent.; and the building trades, 143·4 per cent.

The census elucidated a further noteworthy fact—the steady and rapid tendency towards the centralisation of industry. "This takes two directions," says the report. "On the one hand, large concerns of 500, 1000, and more workpeople gain more and more ascendency. Their number increases every year, and to a large extent they swallow up the dependent business of all kinds. The larger embroidery manufacturer has his lithographer, his bookbinder, his cabinet-maker; the printer includes in his business every possible branch of the polygraphic arts, and has, too, his typefounder and his bookbinders. This tendency is visible on all hands, and as if that were not enough, it drives everything to special industrial centres, and especially to the towns. This is a factor which cannot be ignored if one would understand the course of development which Swiss industry is following more and more."

On the whole the female operatives had nominally decreased relatively—the percentage of the whole in 1888 was 45·8, and in 1895 40·5—but in reality they had increased. That is, in every industry in which women are employed their number proportionally to that of men was larger as compared with 1888, and only a large increase of workpeople in industries exclusively employing men caused the general ratio to be otherwise. In some industries—especially the textile—the increase had been as high as 3 and 4 per cent., with the result that from 51 to 82 per cent. (in various branches) of the total employees were women and girls.

As to nationality the workpeople fell to the following countries—Swiss 174,697 (87·0 per cent. of the whole); Germans 14,872 (7·4 per cent.); French 3354 (1·7 per cent.); Italians 5124 (2·6 per cent.); Austrians 1896 (0·9 per cent.); English 36 (0·01 per cent.); other lands 220 (0·1 per cent.); 12·7 per cent. of the whole factory operatives were aliens.

As to age, 14·3 per cent. of the workers were under 18 years, 76·7 per cent. between 18 and 50 years, and 9 per cent. over 50. The actual figures were: from 14 to 18 years, 13,170 males and 15,442 females; from 18 to 50 years, 93,133 males and 60,352 females; over 50 years, 12,901 males and 5201 females.

It was found also that more than half the factory population worked the full maximum number of 65 hours. In the textile industry in general 83 per cent. worked the maximum hours, and in the cotton-spinning industry 100 per cent. The figures were :—

No. of hours.	No. of operatives.	Percentage of the whole.
54 and under	3,963	2·0
From 54 to 57......	6,651	3·3
,, 57 to 60......	56,738	28·4
,, 60 to 62½ ...	18,530	9·3
,, 62½ to 65......	114,297	57·0
	200,179	100·0

It must be added, however, that there is a gradual tendency to reduce the hours of work. In the second circuit there were at the end of the year 1893 702 concerns working 11 hours a day, and 238 10 hours, while in June, 1895, the numbers were respectively 603 and 440. Many concerns work 11 hours in summer and 9, 9½, and 10 in winter. The question of a reduced normal work-day is, indeed, one of the more urgent of Swiss labour questions, and in a number of trades it is being persistently agitated.

The question of overtime and nightwork is also a burning one. It is commonly complained that permission to work overtime is given upon very insufficient grounds by the local authorities. Certain it is that where it is given sparingly it is not on account of any unwillingness on the part of the employers to take advantage of it. As a rule, however, the extensions allowed are very short,—an hour or less a day in 50 per cent. of the cases. The official returns also show that many applications to work overtime and on Sundays are not granted. Thus in the canton of Zurich during 1895 51 concerns were allowed to work overtime, while 24 applications were rejected; and four applications to work on Sundays were granted where 14 were refused. Again, in the autumn of 1895, when the number of unemployed in the watchmaking trade was unusually large, the Governments of Berne and Neuchâtel discontinued altogether the permission to work overtime in that industry, with a view to equalising employment somewhat.

The wages paid to the Swiss working classes fall much below the standard common in this country in spite of the longer hours worked. That there is great room for improvement here is proved by the fact that quite recently the silk-ribbon weavers of Basle struck work for minimum wages of 3s. 4d. per day; the coopers of Lucerne struck for minimum wages of 3s. 9d. per day; and the masons of Basle for 4s. per day; while the carpenters and builders of Berne threatened to strike for a normal pay of 4½d. an hour or 3s. 9d. per day, which was amicably conceded.

The success of such strikes in Switzerland, where there is not the powerful Trade Union organisation which is found in England, would be far oftener uncertain than is the case were it not for the influence of the democratic spirit prevalent, which is said to

cause the public to take sides with the strikers
almost as a matter of course, and sometimes without
regard to the rights and wrongs of the dispute.   As
a strike oddity may be mentioned an incident which
occurred during a strike of watchmakers in the
canton of Soleure in the spring of 1895.   When the
struggle was at its height the Communal Assembly
of one village affected voted £20 a week to the support of the strikers.   The employers appealed to the
Cantonal Government, which ruled that the Commune was within its rights so long as help was not
withheld from other destitute or needy persons not
concerned in the dispute.

It would be wrong to conclude, however, that industrial difficulties are commoner in Switzerland
than elsewhere.   Some figures upon the duration of
service in the third circuit, recently prepared by the
Factory Inspector, attest not only friendly relationships, but the attachment of the Swiss workman to
his home.   Of the employees in the cotton-spinning
mills of this circuit 10·2 per cent. had worked from
20 to 30 years in the same concerns, 3·6 per cent.
from 30 to 40 years, 1·3 per cent. from 40 to 50 years,
and 0·3 per cent. over 50 years.   In the cotton-weav-
ing mills 17·4 per cent. had worked from 20 to 30
years in the same concerns, 3·8 from 30 to 40, 0·8
from 40 to 50, and 0·2 over 50; and equal percentages were shown by other industries.

A wages return prepared by the Inspector of the

second circuit in 1895 shows that wages were paid as
follows as to frequency in his seven cantons:—

Canton.	Weekly.	Fortnightly.	Monthly.
Berne	45	119	87
Freiburg	10	24	22
Ticino	11	27	25
Vaud	63	150	77
Neuchâtel	93	125	70
Geneva	64	129	59
Valais	3	6	13
Total	289	580	353

The long terms of payment are found to lead to an
excessive resort to credit amongst working people, to
whom it is a source both of hardship and loss. In
95 per cent. of the foregoing cases Saturday was the
pay-day. The plan of keeping wages in hand is
likewise a hardship. There is also much complaint
on the score of improper deductions, and the Inspector of the first circuit says in his last report
that in the hands of certain of the embroidery manufacturers the system of deductions has become one of
pure robbery, as the best cure for which he counsels
full public exposure of the offenders.

It is universally agreed that far more accidents
occur in the factories and other concerns under legal
oversight than there should be with ordinary care,
and the Inspectors complain of the neglect—in some

cases deliberate and wanton—of many employers to adopt preventive measures, even against such a grave contingency as that of fire. For purpose of comparison, the return of accidents notified for the whole country in 1894 is given:

Factory circuit.	In factories.	In other concerns.	Total.	No. of workpeople employed.	Compensation paid. Francs.
1st circuit ...	3,880	2,425	6,305	82,647	969,547
2nd „ ...	1,418	1,407	2,825	36,931	393,926
3rd „ ...	3,144	2,409	5,553	80,621	785,127
No. of accidents	8,442	6,241	14,683	200,199	2,148,600

The Inspectors also state that the claims for compensation give rise to much unnecessary dispute, owing to fault on both sides. While the employers often seek to escape liability, workpeople at times make unconscionable demands, and deception is not uncommon. The case is related in the report for 1895 of a man who claimed remuneration for a host of superfluous visits which he had paid to an injured son in a distant hospital, and a machinist's ground of action was alleged blood-poisoning caused by machine oil. It is a noteworthy fact that a larger number of accidents fall on Monday than on any other day of the week. Herr Rauschenbach reports that in 1894 the accidents in the factories in his district fell as follows, as to percentage:—Monday, 19·3; Tuesday, 16·1; Wednesday, 15·7; Thursday, 15·6; Friday,

14·9; Saturday, 16·9; Sunday, 1·5. In concerns other than factories the accidents fell as follows:— Monday, 17·6; Tuesday, 15·4; Wednesday, 17·0; Thursday, 16·3; Friday, 14·9; Saturday, 16·5; Sunday, 2·2. In the aggregate:—Monday, 18·6; Tuesday, 15·9; Wednesday, 16·2; Thursday, 15·9; Friday, 14·9; Saturday, 16·7; Sunday, 1·8. As to season, the month most fruitful in accidents in factories is December, with 9·5 per cent. of the whole; and the month most free is March, with 7·5 per cent. In other concerns the worst month is May (when, however, there is most work), with 10 per cent.; and the best are January and February, when work is slack, with 6 per cent.

It ought to be stated that there is on the part of the working classes, especially in the larger industrial centres, a certain dissatisfaction at the manner in which some of the provisions of the Factory Act are disregarded by employers, and I learned that secret committees of operatives exist in a number of towns charged with the duty of watching the Act. Cases of infraction are reported to them, and they in turn communicate either with the Factory Inspectors, the Workmen's Secretary, or other competent officials. Sufficient has been said to demonstrate that the dissatisfaction spoken of is not altogether groundless.

CHAPTER II

THE principal defect of the Federal Factory Act consists in its limitations ; it does not go far enough. This is the opinion not merely of ardent social reformers, but of most of the cantonal legislatures, some of which have made a serious endeavour to make up for the Act's shortcomings. In the first place, it ignores the multitudinous home industries, which yet give employment to over a hundred thousand persons—men, women, and children. These industries are entirely beyond the pale of the federal law so far as regards the restriction of the hours of work and the healthiness (or otherwise) of the places of work. Everybody is conscious of the gravity of this defect, but for various reasons—the chief being the inherent difficulties of the case—no attempt has yet been made to deal with the question upon national lines. Then, too, the Factory Act fails to control the trades and smaller industries in which the workers of a single concern are few in number,

20

and particularly those whose workers are exclusively or chiefly women and girls.

It is from the latter standpoint—protection for female workpeople—that the cantons, in their individual action, have mostly viewed the deficiencies of federal legislation and have passed supplementary measures. Perhaps the credit for having made the first move belongs to the canton of Basle-Urban, which regulated the hours of working women so long ago as 1884. The little canton of Obwalden, however, led the way with a comprehensive measure, when in 1887 (April 24) it enacted protection for both male and female workers. The canton of Basle-Urban closely followed with a law of April 23, 1888; Glarus came next with a law of May 8, 1892; St. Gall with one of May 18, 1893; Zurich with one of August 12, 1894; while the cantons of Neuchâtel, Glarus, and Geneva afforded apprentices protection by laws of November 21, 1890, May 8, 1892, and October 15, 1892, respectively. At the present time the cantons of Lucerne, Vaud, and Glarus are engaged upon larger measures. I propose to summarise the provisions of the principal of these laws.

BASLE-URBAN.

The law of this canton for the protection of women (*Gesetz betreffend den Schutz der Arbeiterinnen*) passed in April, 1888, superseded a modest statute of 1884

—whose prime instigator was a Basle manufacturer —which simply regulated the hours of female workers. The later law applies to all trades in which three or more females (*Frauenspersonen*) are "industrially" employed, or in which any girls under eighteen years of age are employed as ordinary workpeople or as apprentices, with the exclusion of licensed houses of refreshment and also shops in so far as the owners of the latter do not employ their workwomen in industrial work, but in serving customers. It is laid down that the daily hours of the workers shall not exceed eleven, and on the eve of Sunday and any festival ten, and these hours must fall between six a.m. and eight p.m. with a mid-day pause of at least an hour. Sunday work is prohibited. Overtime may be permitted temporarily by the Department for the Interior until eleven at the latest, but if desired for more than two weeks together it must be sanctioned by the Government, as also when overtime is sought for more than three weeks during any two months. In any case, however, girls under eighteen years and pregnant women may not work overtime, nor may they in any event work later than eight o'clock. Pregnant women must stay away from work before and after confinement eight weeks altogether, and they can only return on furnishing proof that six weeks have elapsed since childbirth. In the absence of written agreement to the contrary, a fortnight's notice is requisite on either side to the termination of an agreement, this dating from pay-day or Saturday. Only such fines may be imposed as are named in the regulations of the workshop, and have thus received official sanction. They may not at the most exceed half-a-day's wages, and the proceeds must be used for the interest of the work-people. Deductions for spoiled work may only be made where the injury is intentional or the result of culpable negligence. All workshops are placed under the control and regulations of the sanitary authorities.

This law was followed five years later by one on Sunday rest—the *Gesetz betreffend die Sonntagsruhe* of April 13, 1893. The preamble expressly says that it is intended only to cover existing insufficiencies until a federal measure shall be passed. It constitutes the chief ecclesiastical festivals (Good Friday, Easter Day, Whitsuntide, Rogation Day, and Christmas), with all Sundays, New Year's Day, and Ascension Day, public " rest-days " (*Ruhetage*) in the canton. On these days all industrial, agricultural, and other occupations occasioning "noise and disturbance" are prohibited. In commercial concerns (offices and the like) employees and apprentices may not work at all on the high festivals, and on other public rest-days only from half-past ten to twelve o'clock in the forenoon, and every employee and apprentice must be given an entirely free Sunday every fortnight. Shops must be closed all day on

high festivals, and on other public rest-days from
nine to half-past ten in the forenoon; employees and
apprentices, as well as members of the tradesman's
family under fourteen years of age, may only be
employed up to noon, and alternate Sundays must be
entirely free.   Hawking from house to house is prohibited on public rest-days, though food may be
delivered by tradesmen to their customers, and after
half-past ten o'clock the sale of fruit, flowers, and
bakery may take place in public places sanctioned by
the police.   Hunting and sales by auction are also
forbidden on these days.

A number of businesses and occupations are, however, exempted from the foregoing restrictions,
including those of apothecaries, bakers and confectioners, butchers, milk-sellers, hairdressers, gardeners,
with inns, bathing establishments, urgent work so
far as permitted by the police, public means of conveyance, work in concerns which from their nature
require uninterrupted operations, though here, if
they are not subject to the Factory Act, special
sanction is necessary; work in connection with
harvesting, necessary street work, and the care and
feeding of domestic animals.   Likewise on the
statutory rest-days the perambulating of bands of
music and singers and all noisy public processions
are forbidden, as are public performances and amusements between the hours of nine and half-past ten in
the forenoon and all day on every high festival as well

as after three p.m. on the day before. Finally, power is reserved to the Government to moderate the provisions of the law on special occasions, as at *fêtes*, Christmas and New Year time, during fairs, and the like.

St. Gall.

In the new constitution of St. Gall (of November 16, 1890) there was introduced the clause, " The State shall protect the 'labour-power' (*Arbeitskraft*), particularly that of women and children, which is employed in such trades and industries as do not come under the federal legislation." Yet the canton has not done more to give effect to so excellent a principle than some cantons that lacked the spur and encouragement of a constitutional revision.

The law of May 18, 1893,—operative since October 1 of that year—which puts the constitutional theory into concrete form, avows as its object the protection of "female workpeople as well as the employees of both sexes of shops and licensed houses against over-exertion and harm." It is a somewhat weak and inconsistent measure. The first part of the law applies to all businesses, not coming under the Federal Factory Act, in which more than two females work "industrially" for wages, and to all businesses in which female apprentices or girls under eighteen years are employed, with the exception of females engaged in offices or in agriculture. For the protected workpeople included in this definition a normal work-day of eleven hours is fixed, with an hour less on Saturdays and the days preceding public holidays. These hours must fall between six a.m. and eight p.m. with a pause of at least an hour at noon, but women who have households to attend to may leave work half-an-hour sooner. Work on Sundays and public holidays is prohibited. Overtime to a maximum of two hours a day, and extending to ten p.m. at the latest, may be sanctioned in special cases for not longer than fourteen days at once, or more than three months during a year for the same firm, though in extraordinary cases this permission may be relaxed. Women need not, however, work overtime unless they wish, and they must be paid higher wages for it. Pregnant women and likewise girls under eighteen years may not work overtime under any circumstances. The former are afforded exceptional protection. For a period of six weeks they must be " excluded from all industrial work," and in the later stages they may " leave work at any time by mere announcement to that effect." Girls under fourteen years may not be employed in industrial work, and girls under sixteen may not be kept more than three hours together at treadle machines. School hours of whatever kind reckon in their case to the maximum work-day. The period of notice is fourteen days on both sides, and wages must be paid at not longer intervals than a fortnight. Deductions can only be made on account of spoiled work when the injury is the result of intention or negligence, and only such fines can be imposed as have been officially sanctioned; also they cannot exceed one-fourth of a day's wages, and the proceeds must be used for the benefit of the workpeople. There are also provisions to secure the healthiness of the work-rooms.

The second part of the law applies to shop assistants and public-house employees. As to the former no restriction of the daily hours of work is made save that ten hours of uninterrupted rest shall be secured to them. Similarly there is no prohibition of Sunday trading, beyond the requirement that employees who work on that day shall be given an equal amount of free time during the week. The employees of public and refreshment houses do not fare even so well as this. No limitation is placed upon their hours of work save that they shall be allowed eight hours of unbroken rest, and that in return for Sunday service they shall have half-a-day free during the week; for the rest, they may be employed in the evening to the legal hour of closing. Girls under eighteen years who do not belong to the landlord's family may not be employed in regular service.

ZURICH.

The Government of Canton Zurich in 1894 passed a " Law for the Protection of Workwomen " (*Gesetz betreffend den Schutz der Arbeiterinnen*, August 12, 1894), which came into force at the beginning of 1895. Hitherto the federal law had offered protection to some 45,000 factory operatives of the canton, but there remained outside its influence and benefit many industries, both large and small, employing a very large number of women and girls—on a moderate calculation between 4000 and 5000—and for years it had been notorious that in these industries the workers were subject to excessive hours of work, Sunday and night work, unhealthy surroundings, arbitrary treatment in respect of the wages contract and the conditions of discharge, unjustifiable fines and deductions from wages, etc. The law was thus intended to do for those exempted industries what the federal law did for the factory system, yet with the important exceptions of women employed in agricultural occupations, commercial offices, and the hotel and inn industry, for whom special treatment was reserved. Women engaged in house industries also were only affected in so far as they in turn had female employees in their service, as in the case of sempstresses, washerwomen, and laundresses who worked in the homes of employers.

By the new law it is required that all work-rooms

shall be of adequate size, light, dry, well-ventilated, and properly heated when necessary, and in general of such sort that the health of the workers may not suffer. All practicable measures shall also be taken to protect the workers against bodily injury, and these hygienic provisions are placed under the oversight of the local public health authorities. To the normal termination of service a notice of fourteen days is requisite on either side, dating from the pay-day or Saturday, and every worker may on leaving require a certificate setting forth the duration of her service and the character of the work she has done. The law provides that girls under fourteen years of age may neither be employed in regular service nor as apprentices, while women in childbirth must have a month's rest after confinement, and they may remain from work six weeks if they wish. Work on Sundays and festivals is forbidden under all circumstances. For the rest the maximum hours of work are fixed at ten daily (the lowest maximum enacted by any Swiss law)—falling between six a.m. and eight p.m.— but nine on the days preceding Sundays and festivals, while the noon pause is fixed at an hour and a half; nor may work be taken home. Where girls under eighteen years of age are liable to attend continuation schools or other instruction (including preparation for confirmation) the hours so employed are to be counted as part of the normal hours of occupation. In the event of an exceptional prolongation of work—

which, however, is absolutely prohibited in the case
of girls under eighteen years of age and cannot be
forced upon the rest except with their free consent—
the maximum is two hours in a day, and the total
excess for the year must not exceed seventy-five hours,
while wages for overtime must be at least twenty-five
per cent. higher than the ordinary rate. Such overtime, moreover, should cease at eight p.m. and may
never extend beyond nine p.m. An employer may
only impose such fines as have been duly approved as
proper to be included in the regulations of his or her
concern, and in no case may a fine exceed one-fourth
of a day's wages, while all fines must be employed
for the benefit of the workpeople generally. These
provisions do not apply to the obligation of employer
and employed in respect of injury for which compensation may be claimed at law.

It is a sign of the healthy public sentiment which
prevails on this subject in the canton of Zurich that
the law was approved by an overwhelming majority
of the voting citizens. When the *referendum* was
taken on August 12, 1894, 45,909 votes were given
for the measure against 12,531 against.

Zurich is now enacting a law regulating trades
generally (*Gesetz betreffend das Gewerbewesen*). The
law applies to all handicrafts, trades, and industries
which do not come under the federal law with the
exception of agriculture. It also subjects the trades
of porters, cabmen, boat pliers, and public conveyers

generally, as well as service and information agents and chimney-sweepers, to municipal control.

Employers are required to adopt all practicable measures for the protection of the health and life of their workpeople, and dangerous industries and trades are subjected to special police control. The public generally are also thought of, for it is forbidden to establish any new business concerns which are noisy, which pollute either air, earth, or water, or which perturb the ground, in inhabited localities, save in such as are set apart for this purpose; while existing works are required to adopt all possible precautionary methods and measures with the object of restricting the disadvantages spoken of, and where this cannot be effected by artificial means the local authorities are authorised to require the discontinuance or removal of the work, with due regard to the satisfaction of vested interests.

Industrial work of all kinds is forbidden on Sundays, New Year's Day, Good Friday, Easter Monday, Ascension Day, Whit Monday, and Christmas Day and the day following, and shops are subjected to the same restriction; but exceptions may be made in extraordinary cases—where from the nature of an industry uninterrupted work is necessary, and in the case of trades concerned with the food supply. As regards the last and shops generally the local authorities determine whether the restrictions shall be imposed or not, yet not before the views of the

employees as well as the employers concerned have
been heard and considered. In any event the hours
of work on Sundays and festivals must be so arranged
that public worship shall not be interfered with, and
the entire afternoons shall be free. Yet here again
the hours may be increased on the four Sundays
preceding Christmas Day, with the reservation that
all assistants, workpeople, and apprentices shall have
the third Sunday quite free. Special hours are
fixed for the hair-dressing business.

The duration of work, following the Factory Act, is
fixed at sixty-four hours a week, and the provisions of
that Act as to night-work are also applied. All overtime and night and Sunday work must at least be
reckoned twenty-five per cent. higher; wages must
be paid at no longer interval than a fortnight, and the
truck system is prohibited. Deductions for the rent,
cleaning, heating, and lighting of the workshops and
for the use of tools are prohibited ; and raw materials
and material negligently spoiled must be charged for
at cost price. An employer is empowered to retain
six days' wages in hand, but no more. On leaving
service an employee or workman may require a
written certificate of the character and duration of
his work. When an employee is killed or seriously
injured at his work the employer must immediately
notify the fact to the local police authorities, whose
duty it is to institute an inquiry into the whole
circumstances and to report to the *Statthalter* or

Governor, who completes the investigation. Workshop regulations must be approved by the Government, and the workpeople concerned must be given an opportunity of stating their views regarding them. No fines can be imposed which are not authorised by such regulations; they cannot in any one case exceed one-half of a day's wages; and the proceeds must be employed in the interest of the workpeople.

The provisions dealing especially with employees in offices prohibit work on Sundays and festivals, emergencies excepted, and fix the weekly work-time at fifty-four hours, though periodical extensions are permissible, with the sanction of the local government body if for a period not exceeding two weeks, and of the Government if for longer. Salaries must be paid at least monthly, on the last day of the month.

Other provisions deal with the training of apprentices, and the provision of industrial and mercantile continuation schools, which latter may be either carried on by the State or by local government bodies, trade societies, or private persons with the help of the State.

VAUD.

The canton of Vaud is now (1897) passing a law for the protection of workpeople (*loi sur la protection des ouvriers*), which is intended in the same way to supplement the federal factory legislation. The law

D

is largely based on the regulations introduced in the cantons of Zurich, Basle, St. Gall, and Glarus, and one of its distinguishing merits is that, like the supplementary laws of the last-named canton and of Obwalden, it applies to both sexes. As the law was expected to pass substantially in the form which it took at the time these pages were in the press, it will not be amiss to summarise its provisions. Like the law of Zurich it applies to the workpeople of all concerns in the protected industries and pursuits, irrespective of the numbers they may employ. With the exception of agriculture and offices, it embraces all industries, handicrafts, and trades which are exempted from federal legislation. Thus even the house industry is here included, though domestic service is excluded. First it requires employers to adopt suitable measures to protect the health of their workpeople, by the provision of sanitary surroundings, and to prevent accidents. The duration of work may not exceed twelve hours a day or sixty-five a week, and in the middle of the day there must be a pause of an hour, but those workpeople who have household duties or who do not take their mid-day meal in the proximity of the workshop may have a pause of two hours. No minimum age is prescribed in the employment of children, which is a distinct defect of the law, nor are the provisions as to hours applicable to attendants (*personnes employées à servir la clientèle*), as clerks, shop-girls, waitresses, waiters in *cafés*, servants in inns, etc. In the case of juveniles, however, the time devoted to primary, technical, and religious instruction is to be reckoned to the legal work-day. There must be nine hours of rest at night, and work may not be carried on later than eleven o'clock. Sunday work is prohibited as a rule, but to meet the case of hotels and the like the law stipulates that another day or two half-days may be taken for the weekly rest instead. In exceptional cases overtime may, however, be worked by per-mission of the local authority, and the Council of State may authorise departures from the normal work-time regulations where the special conditions of an industry may seem to require it. Women in childbirth must remain from work for four weeks after confinement, and this time may be extended to six weeks if they choose. Girls under eighteen years who are neither the children nor the relatives of the licensees may not be employed in drinking houses. In general wages must be paid every fortnight, unless there be a written agreement to the contrary. Deductions for the rent, cleaning, lighting, and heat-ing of the work-room, for the hire and use of tools, and for insurance are prohibited, nor may more than a week's wages be kept in hand. No penalties may be imposed which are not embodied in regulations approved by the local authority. The maximum shall be one-fourth of a day's wages; and all proceeds from this source must be applied in the interest of the workpeople. Should the employer supply food, lodging, or material it must be at cost price. Infraction of the law, the execution of which is to be entrusted to the local authorities, subject to the control of the Department for Agriculture and Commerce, may be visited by a penalty as high as £20.

CHAPTER III

THE HOUSE INDUSTRIES [1]

IT has long been recognised by all thoughtful sociologists that the problem of rural migration is only a part of the wider and graver problem of unemployment. That factors besides lack of work help to feed the constant stream of population which flows from country to town is, of course, admitted. The superior attractions offered by the town, in diversity, conditions, and remuneration of employment, as well as in social amenities, certainly account for no small portion of the rural exodus. None the less, the rural employment question is essentially one not of kind but of degree, not of quality but of quantity : if those on the land had plenty to do and a decent return for doing it, the overgrowth of our towns would speedily receive a salutary check.

In Switzerland rural migration is counteracted, in some measure, by a remarkable system of house industries, which, while in part a survival of a

[1] Reprinted from the *Economic Journal* by permission of the editors.

primitive form of production, still plays a most
important part in the economic life of the nation.
A belief that the house-industrial system might
throw some light upon the treatment of our own
rural difficulties led me to undertake inquiries in
various parts of the country, beginning at the seat
of government, where such official guidance as was
available was readily afforded me. The results of
my investigations on the spot were supplemented by
information which was only to be obtained by letter,
so that my conclusions are hardly open to the danger
of over-generalisation. At the same time it need
hardly be said that no full and particular dissertation
upon the entire system of home or house industry is
here attempted. Not only so, but such industries
as are followed in rural districts have in the main
been dealt with. Except where indications to the
contrary appear, my own observations are to be
accepted with this restriction.

I.—EXTENT OF THE HOUSE INDUSTRIES.

A word may be premised as to the present extent
of this primitive system of production. In attempting
an enumeration of the house-industrial population
one is confronted by serious difficulties. In the first
place, no official statistics on the subject exist, since
the house industries do not come under the federal
factory legislation, and the Inspectors of Factories

thus possess absolutely no jurisdiction respecting them. But a further difficulty consists in the inevitably indefinite and arbitrary division between house industries proper and handicrafts. This has been recognised at each census, and the introduction to the returns for 1888 observes :—

"The house industries, or at least a large part of them, present such a mixture of independence and dependence that any distinction must inevitably be artificial, and even then it cannot be regarded as corresponding to the real facts of the case."[1]

The only way of arriving at an estimate of the population employed in the house industries—and then it can only be approximate—is by deducting the number of workpeople of individual trades enumerated in the special Factory Statistics from the aggregate number in the same trades returned in the general census. By following this deductive method (taking the respective returns for 1888), Herr Rauschenbach, Federal Factory Inspector for the Third Circuit, has kindly supplied me with the figures for the principal industries, given in the table on the next page.

Other industries of less extent are match-box-making (a speciality of the Frutigerthal), shoemaking, which is carried on in the cantons of Soleure and Aargau, where the people work at home for the

---

[1] *Die Ergebnisse der Volkszählung vom 1ten December*, 1888 (III.). Zurich: Füssli, 1894.

large warehouses; linen-thread-making, and cigar-making.

EMPLOYED IN THE HOUSE INDUSTRIES.

Industry.	Male.	Female.	Total.	Percentage of the total workers.
Watch and clock industry	22,421	10,019	32,440	73·0
Embroidery.............	11,565	15,845	27,410	60·0
Silk	7,085	25,710	37,795	—
Cotton-weaving	3,486	3,256	6,742	—
Straw goods	584	5,219	5,803	86·0
Knitted goods.........	315	3,828	4,143	65·0
To which may be added :—				
Pottery and tiles ...	1,556	62	1,618	67·0
Musical instruments.	922	539	1,461	70·0
Hat-making	733	467	1,200	84·0
Wood-carving, etc....	1,545	107	1,652	95·0
Wicker-work	1,926	269	2,195	100·0

II.—PRESENT POSITION : EFFECT OF TECHNICAL EDUCATION.

Save for local and temporary depression here and there the house industries would appear to be maintaining their ground well. This is largely owing to the co-operative efforts which the Federal Government, the Cantonal Governments, and the Communes are making to multiply trade and industrial schools. The application of technical instruction to the house industries, upon which so large a part of the rural population relies for a subsistence, has undoubtedly been productive of immense good.

Here some general remarks from two of the Federal Inspectors of Factories may be quoted. Dr. Schuler (of the First Circuit) says :—

"It is difficult to say whether an industry of this kind is really on the decline in the rural districts. For years this was believed of the silk industry, but in the recent favourable years there has been great activity in this industry. The embroidery branch has perhaps diminished as a house industry more than any other. The industry next worst off in this respect is the clock and watch industry; coloured weaving is also in a very bad position. At the present time the industry most favourably circumstanced is the silk industry."

Herr Rauschenbach's testimony is very decisive. He writes :—

"Though the most important of these industries —embroidery and watchmaking—which are both carried on in factories and at home, may have passed their highest point, it is in no sense possible to speak of decay. In the embroidery industry, indeed, the remarkable process is going on of factories giving way to the house industry, though in the watch industry the opposite is the case."

Doubtless much of the vitality of the house-industrial system is due to the singular tenacity with which the workers hold to their particular industry.

In part this may be attributed to natural preference
and traditional ties, in part to the fact that in many
of the industries considerable aptitude is requisite,
which aptitude is only acquired after years of hard
apprenticeship, in part to the seclusion of many of
the valleys in which home industries are carried on,
the difficulty of migration, and uncertainty as to the
success which might attend the bold adventurer who
forsook the calling and home of his fathers for the
busier life offered in towns. A further reason is the
strong attachment of the Switzer to his native soil—
by which must be understood, not federal territory
indiscriminately, but the canton and even the parish
in which he was born. For after all, the banal
appeal to the "longing of the Swiss peasant for his
native mountains" is by no means mere rhetorical
moonshine, as the men who killed William Tell
would have us believe. A passage in so prosaic a
document as a recent report of the Brienz Carving
School is evidence in point, for therein, I note, the
director laments that one of the students had to be
sent home to his native Simmenthal on account of
"insuperable home sickness, which incapacitated him
from doing any continuous work." The Simmenthal,
be it added, lies in the same canton, near to Lake
Thun, and it is only an hour's journey from Brienz.

Upon the subject of the house-workers' attachment
to their traditional occupation, a letter received from
Dr. Schuler says :—

" The house - workers hold with extraordinary
tenacity to their calling. . . . Only protracted
hunger causes them to turn their backs upon their
accustomed occupation, and even then they return
to it as soon as possible. This was the case in the
embroidery branch."

Yet in general the livelihood to be made in the
house industries—at least in the rural districts—is a
very modest one, though it is important to remember
that the standard of life common amongst Swiss
workers as a whole is not high. Not only so, but
the strain upon physical strength is often unduly
severe. The house industries being exempted from
the Factory Laws, they are not subject to restrictions
upon the hours of labour, and these hours as a
consequence are long and disproportionate to the
earnings. In the case of house-workers who are
employed in their homes by middlemen, the number
of hours worked depends largely on the amount of
work there is to do, and this may fluctuate greatly
with the seasons. When work is abundant twelve,
fourteen, and even sixteen hours will be " put in "
during the day by men and women alike, and it is
a common cause of complaint that young children
are also required to do their share in the evening.
In two places I was informed that the school authorities, while very friendly disposed towards the house
industries in general, were dissatisfied with the want
of legislative control in this respect. Where a house-

worker unites the functions at once of capital and
labour, and especially where raw material is cheap
—as, for example, in the wood-carving and pottery
industries, in which a large number of the workpeople
are independent of employers—long hours are almost
invariable, for here there is every inducement to
over-production. In such cases work frequently
begins with the light of day, and with the smallest
intermission continues until sundown, and sometimes
far into the night.

Nevertheless, work is not equally intensive.
Many of the operations incidental to the house
industries are such as can be taken up, put down,
and again resumed at will, and in the case of women
perhaps fit in conveniently with domestic duties of
the ordinary kind. The absence of compulsion—
save such as is imposed by prudence or the needs of
the day—and also of control tends also to relieve
the weight of rural toil. Certainly it is not difficult
to pronounce between the desirableness, from a
purely hedonistic standpoint, of the lot of the urban
operative, immured from morning till evening within
the walls of a great factory, in which work proceeds
by military rule and often under pressure of inordin-
ately quickly-driven machinery, and that of the
Swiss hand-weaver, say, who pursues his work without rest, maybe, yet without haste, or of his wife
at home, who placidly knits or plaits in the open air
over neighbourly chat.

III.—Effect upon Emigration.

It would naturally be expected of the house industries, if they are efficient at all, that, combined with pastoral pursuits as they often are, they would checkmate the inroad of industry upon agriculture and lessen migration and emigration, and I believe that both these effects are produced to a substantial degree. As to the first, it is undoubtedly true that in Switzerland, as in other countries, industry has of late years occupied ground previously held by agriculture, yet there has been nothing like the displacement that has been noticeable elsewhere. The agricultural and non-agricultural sections of the population at the last three enumerations have been as follows :

	AGRICULTURAL.					NON-AGRICULTURAL.
1870	...	1,111,491	...	...	...	1,543,510
1880	...	1,113,407	...	...	...	1,718,380
1888	...	1,092,827	...	...	...	1,824,927

Decrease in 18 years, 18,664   Increase in 18 years, 281,417

It is noteworthy, however, that the decrease of the agricultural population—after all, very slight—has been exclusively where agriculture and industry have been mixed, while the agricultural population in overwhelmingly pastoral districts has really increased.

The extent to which agriculture continues to be followed, either exclusively or partially, appears from the fact that in 89 of the 182 administrative districts into which the country is divided, 50 per cent. or more of the population was employed pastorally in 1888, while the proportion for the whole country was 40 per cent.

The following are the percentages according to canton :—

PERCENTAGE OF THE POPULATION ENGAGED IN AGRICULTURE.

Valais	78	Schaffhausen		44
Obwalden	63	Berne		43
Freiburg	60	Thurgau		40
Uri	59	Zug		37
Grisons	58	Appenzell (Int.)		37
Ticino	54	Soleure		35
Lucerne	54	Basle (Rural)		31
Vaud	49	St. Gall		30
Nidwalden	47	Zurich		29
Schwyz	47	Appenzell (Ext.)		21
Aargau	46	Geneva		14
Glarus	27	Basle (Urban)		3
Neuchâtel	18			

Obviously it would be impossible to attempt exact statistical proof of the efficacy of the house industries in checking emigration. That they do, however, minimise emigration, by counteracting some of its more potent causes, as they operate in this and other countries, cannot seriously be doubted. Besides the local testimony which has already been given or remains yet to be cited, I have been favoured with the written opinions of two of the three Federal Factory Inspectors. It will be observed that one opinion is far less reserved than the other. Dr. Schuler writes :—

"I scarcely believe that it can be assumed that

our house industries prevent emigration, particularly amongst the rural population. Servants of both sexes are in such great demand, and are in parts so well paid, that agriculture suffers from lack of labour. A very large number of them are foreigners, and this is the case likewise with out-door workers, especially masons. These occupations would, therefore, employ a large number of Swiss, even if the house industries should decay. Nor do I believe that the collapse of isolated house industries has occasioned any considerable permanent increase of emigration. For the time being this may have been the case, but far oftener the consequence has been the transference of labour to the factory industry or to the towns."

Yet in my opinion the view here expressed does not sufficiently appreciate either the great numerical and economic importance of the house industries, or the fact that the factory system is even now only partially nationalised in Switzerland. Of the 1,225,346 persons of both sexes who were classified in 142 avocations in the occupation census of 1888, only 158,506, or 13 per cent., worked in factories. It is evident that a long time must elapse, even under conditions favourable to its development, before the factory system can hope to swallow up the older house system.

Herr Rauschenbach takes a different view from his colleague. He observes :—

" That these industries somewhat check emigration

appears from the fact that in the period 1887—1891, in which on the whole 37,157 persons emigrated, only 2·5 per cent. of the emigrants belonged to the watch-making, 2·2 per cent. to the textile, and 1 per cent. to the embroidery industry, while 46·6 per cent. fell to agriculture. How far the emigrants belonged to the house and factory industries respectively it is impossible to determine."

Upon the same point I had an opportunity, while in Berne, of conversing with Herr Dreifuss, the head of the Federal Emigration Bureau. He had not made any systematic attempt to determine the connection between the house industries and emigration, but he pointed out an interesting fact which he had established and had emphasised in his last annual report. It is this :—

" The less settled part of the population shows a greater disposition to emigrate than do people who were born in the cantons in which they reside. If we had statistics of emigration according to Communes, it is highly probable that we should find that in the case of inhabitants who do not live in the Communes in which they are domiciled, the inclination to emigrate and the motive for emigration exist in far higher degree than with those who reside in their native parishes."

It is difficult, however, to draw from these words, without unduly forcing them, any other moral than the importance of preserving the existing house industries as far as possible in a healthy state.

I am bound to say that Herr Greulich, the Swiss Workmen's Secretary,[1] takes a somewhat unfavourable view :—

"I do not believe," he writes, "that the house industries are able to prevent the emigration of the rural population, since on the one hand they offer only small earnings, while, on the other, occupation is variable, and some of these industries are decaying; at least, this is the case with the silk industry and embroidery in Canton Zurich. In this canton the silk hand-weaving industry has decidedly fallen off, and has been transferred to where people are satisfied with less wages, while the better paid machine-weaving industry has made progress. It is true that in purely agricultural districts there is greater emigration than elsewhere, yet it also exists in districts having house industries, and only in manufacturing districts does the population increase."

Here, too, it is only fair to remember that Herr Greulich is, in common with the leaders of the organised industrial classes, opposed to the house-industrial system on principle.

After all, this question must be regarded as one not of opinion merely but of fact, and the following table will therefore be of service. It shows the populations of the cantons in 1888, the number of

[1] See Chapter IV., pp. 60—68.

E

Swiss emigrants from each canton, and the rate of the latter per 1000 of the population. The general emigration-rate of 1·78 seems very favourable when compared with the rate for the United Kingdom, which (taking only emigrants of British and Irish nationality), was in 1893 nearly 6 per 1000.

Cantons.	Population (1888).	No. of Swiss emigrants.	Rate per 1000 of population.
Valais	101,985	196	1·9
Obwalden	15,043	73	5·0
Freiburg	119,155	33	0·3
Uri	17,249	38	2·2
Grisons	94,810	259	2·7
Ticino	126,751	536	4·2
Lucerne	135,360	92	0·7
Vaud	247,655	536	4·2
Nidwalden	12,538	17	1·4
Schwyz	50,307	168	3·3
Aargau	193,580	242	1·2
Schaffhausen	37,783	107	3·0
Berne	536,679	1,401	2·6
Thurgau	104,678	134	1·2
Zug	23,029	24	1·0
Appenzell (Int.)	12,888	4	0·3
Soleure................	85,621	123	1·4
Basle (Rural)	61,941	141	2·3
St. Gall	228,174	336	1·4
Zurich	337,183	489	1·4
Appenzell (Ext.)......	54,109	100	2·0
Neuchâtel	108,153	192	1·8
Glarus	33,825	124	3·6
Geneva	105,509	79	0·7
Basle (Urban).........	73,749	177	2·4
All Switzerland	2,917,754	5,621	1·78

IV.—Special Industries Considered.

But this latter branch of the subject may, perhaps, be better illustrated by reference to distinct industries, and their effect upon the populations locally employed. I may name first straw-working, which belongs to the more important branches of house industry. Of 6799 persons employed in the entire straw industry in Switzerland in 1888 (the latest year for which statistics are available), no fewer than 5803 followed it more or less in their homes. This is also peculiarly a woman's industry, for of the latter number, men and boys together only make a meagre 504. The industry is carried on in various parts of Canton Aargau, and largely in the neighbourhood of Wohlen, where it is the staple support of the population. Forty years ago, I was informed, Wohlen was a notoriously poor village, now it is a community of some 2000 souls, and the entire appearance of the place bespeaks prosperity. The houses are well-built, each with its separate garden; there is a handsome suite of elementary schools; a convenient town-hall rises in the centre of the village, which can also boast of the electric light as a public illuminant. The people live well, dress well, are both fond of pleasure and able to indulge in it, and withal they place considerable sums in the savings bank. This happy state of things, I was assured, had entirely resulted from the growth of the straw industry, which employs a large part of the people, either at home or in one or other of the works which have been set up in recent years. There is little emigration, save of the enterprising, the adventurous, and the discontented. A considerable number of children are engaged in the industry, which they prefer to hand labour. They are trained at home while very young, and even during school years are often required to supplement the earnings of their parents by performing the simpler operations.

Wohlen possesses no technical school, but there are schools of the kind elsewhere in the canton. The headmaster of one of the oldest, that at Lenzburg, which is likewise situated in the straw-goods district, writes to me :—

"Our artisans' school exists for the handicrafts, not for large manufactories, and has from forty to fifty pupils. Nearly all the masters send their apprentices to the school in compliance with a compulsory law dating from the summer of 1895. The influence of the school is favourable in that it prepares young people better for their trades than do the ordinary elementary schools. The straw industry is particularly carried on in this neighbourhood. Entire families, even to the little day scholars, are engaged in straw work the whole day through, and often until late in the night, splitting the stalks, and plaiting them for the factories. Few men are employed. In the entire (administrative) district several thousand persons—nearly all women and children—follow this industry, the chief seats of which are Wohlen and Musterschwanden. At the end of September, 1895, work was very plentiful, and women and girls found occupation both all day and in the evening. In consequence of the prosperity of this industry we have no longer any great emigration. In former times, when the industry was depressed, many families crossed the ocean."

The Brienz wood-carving industry, of which probably most visitors to the Bernese Oberland have heard, is likewise a signal example of the vitality of the house-industrial system, and of its ability to provide a normal rural population with remunerative employment.[1] The teacher of the local wood-carving school spoke unequivocally of the immense good done by the industry in the provision of employment for skilled labour, in the creation of a fair average standard of well-being and comfort amongst the lake population, and in the prevention of emigration. "What should we do without our industry?" he remarked. "It keeps the men in work, and allows all who wish it to stay at home instead of seeking a livelihood elsewhere. Without the wood-carving industry the people would have to emigrate wholesale. Not only do we keep our own population, but other people come from different parts of the country, learn

[1] See Chapter XXIII., pp. 266—274.

the industry at our school, and settle here for good. I myself am an outsider."

A letter since received from the teacher of the small wood-carvers' drawing school at Brienzwyler, a village near Brienz, is to the same effect. "The industry," it runs, "is at present growing. On the whole we regard the house industry as advantageous."

The fact may also be added, for what it is worth, that while the permanent pauper class of the whole canton of Berne is equal to 44 per 1000 of the population, the proportion for the administrative district of Interlaken (the eighth district in size of the twenty-two into which the canton is divided), which comprises the seat of the wood-carving industry, is only 28 per 1000, while that for Brienz and Brienz-wyler together is 31.

As the wood-carving industry of the lake of Brienz is a convincing example of the beneficial influence of technical instruction applied to house industry, an example of the decrepitude which follows the absence, or at least the inefficiency, of such instruction is furnished by the pottery industry of the Heimberg valley, in the same canton. The pottery and tile industry belongs to the smaller of the house industries. In 1888 it afforded employment to 2420 persons (2258 males and 162 females), of whom 1618 (1556 males and 62 females) might be reckoned to the house industry. Heimberg is one of the more important centres, and here I was assured that from

300 to 400 persons are employed. Many of these,
however, follow agriculture as well. The moulding
and burning are in general done by the men, the
painting and enamelling by women and girls.
The industry is an old one in Heimberg, dating some
seventy years back. There are several small factories,
but most of the potters work at home, and all the
operations of their craft, from the preparation of
the clay to burning, are done under one roof, the
appliances used being naturally of the simplest
possible character. Besides domestic utensils of a
general kind, and rude country ware, art goods are
largely produced—majolica in particular. There is
a considerable sale locally and to visitors, but the
large business towns, Geneva, Basle, Berne, etc.,
purchase the bulk of the goods. The ordinary
working hours are ten and twelve daily, and the
wages paid to dependent workers are: men, three and
four francs a day; women, two francs. The industry
is at present in a stationary if not in a retrograde
condition, a circumstance which may probably be
attributed to the absence of proper art training.
A "Drawing School for Ceramics" (*Zeichnungschule
für Keramic*) does, indeed, exist in name at Heimberg, but its career has not been successful, notwith-
standing that it is able to draw help from the
Confederation, the canton, and the parish. The
course of instruction lasts six years, freehand drawing
being taken for four years at the elementary school,

and painting (by girls) and modelling (by boys) for two years thereafter. No school-fees are asked, and to the children of poor parents drawing materials are supplied free. The teacher appeared at the time of my visit to be despondent, in so much that he had laid down his post as corypheus of art, and turned village innkeeper instead. All that is needed, however, would seem to be the cultivation of artistic taste in the ornamentation of the pottery. At present it is utterly crude and resourceless. So re-invigorated the industry is capable of great things.

The attitude of the urban working classes towards the house industries I found to be a hostile one, though this can hardly be wondered at. One reason is the lowness of the wages earned, for the effect is to depress wages in the towns, and by spurring the workers to over-production, to create "ruinous competition with the employees of the factory industries, restricted as the latter are as to the hours of work and as to the employment of child-labour." (I quote the closing words from Dr. Schuler's letter.) Another reason for this unfriendliness lies in the fact that the house-industrial system is the *bête noire* and the despair of trade-unionism, even of the somewhat lax and undeveloped type which prevails in Switzerland. Though associations of house-workers do exist, organisation is a matter of extreme difficulty, owing to the scattered character of the industries geographically, and the difficulty, and indeed impossibility, of creating the desirable feeling of solidarity.

I was not in the least surprised to hear Dr. Wassilieff, the Secretary of the Union of Working-men's Associations at Berne, speak vigorously in depreciation of house industries in general, though his attitude is also that of the Federal Workmen's Secretary, who writes to me : " In my opinion it is impossible to re-invigorate the house industry, and it will be a good thing when it is superseded by the factory system. In the country districts it is only a system of sweating."

It is also natural that on the part of officials entrusted with the administration of the Factory Act, there should be hostility to a system of industry which is entirely outside the law, and which in regard alike to conditions of labour and the employment of women and children, involves drawbacks and blemishes which are not tolerated in the inspected factories and workshops.

V.—CONCLUSIONS.

Perhaps my own conclusions will already have been anticipated. To recapitulate briefly, in spite of inevitable defects, I do not regard the house industries as by any means inherently objectionable, from the economic and social standpoint. This is waiving altogether the fact that the best justification of these industries is the prominent place which they occupy in the economic life of the country, and their undoubted efficiency in the past. It is true that wages are lower than in the factory industry, but on the other hand there are compensating advantages in the greater freedom enjoyed by the workers, and in the fact that the house system of employment does not make that sinister inroad upon family life which is made by the disintegrating influences of the urban factory industry. I am also convinced that the assumption that the abolition of the house industries would be followed, as a matter of course, by the prompt absorption of the workers so employed by the factory system, is an altogether too optimistic view. The peculiar exigencies of agriculture alone require the continuance of these industries, while an easy transition from house to factory worker is utterly impossible owing to geographical conditions. Were that supersession of the house industries which, as I have shown, is ardently desired in some quarters, to come to pass, a vast number of independent existences would be destroyed, and there would be caused an amount of unemployed labour which would constitute, perhaps permanently, a social evil of the first magnitude.

It is also, in my view, unquestionable that these industries materially alleviate the problem of rural migration, and also lessen emigration.

At the same time it is clear that the industries

are at the present time being carried on under un-healthy conditions, especially in regard to the hours of labour and the employment of women and children, and that they cannot long continue to be exempted from legal restrictions. It is evident, however, that the supervision and control which will be exercised in the future will not be the same in form and extent as that now applicable to the utterly dissimilar factory system.

CHAPTER IV

THE Swiss Republic has no Federal Department of State answering exactly to the Labour Department of England, or the Department of Labour of the United States. There is a Department for Industry and Agriculture, but it does not profess to concern itself particularly with questions relating to the working classes, whether these belong to the factory and the handicrafts, or the land. In the lack of such a distinct Ministry of State the unofficial or rather semi-official institution known as the Swiss Workmen's Secretary (*Arbeitersekretariat*) was called into existence ten years ago, and though working under the difficulties which are inseparable from private action it has supplied the vacancy with no small measure of success. The Workmen's Secretary is a unique creation without parallel in any other State, and the history of this functionary deserves a prominent place in any record of Swiss experiments in social reform. In August of 1886 the Central Com-

mittee of the Grütliverein, by formal petition, requested the Federal Department for Commerce and
Agriculture (as it was then called) to subsidise a
labour agency which it proposed to establish and to
work in connection with the association, and with
the petition was forwarded the proposed organisation
of the same. It was no innovation, for the Government already contributed towards the salaries
of secretaries who had similarly been appointed
by private organisations to protect the interests of
agriculture, industry, and trade. The Committee at
the same time gave the assurance that the money
which might be voted would not be used in defraying
the administrative expenses of the Grütliverein nor
yet be put to political purposes, but would be
employed solely in the study and furtherance of the
economic interests of the working classes, without
regard to political or sectarian parties and motives.

The petition was received in a friendly and indeed
a cordial manner by the Department, which nine
days later signified its perfect approval of the objects
avowed by the Grütliverein and assented to its
request for State help in their furtherance.

Between that time and the meeting of the Federal
Assembly in autumn the scheme of the Central
Committee expanded. The idea took hold of the
working classes generally throughout the land; other
labour organisations joined hands with the Grütliverein, and it was determined that the projected

Labour Bureau should partake of a national character. To this the Government also agreed, and before the end of the year the desired subvention had been sanctioned, the amount for the first year being fixed at 5000 francs (£200). The Government, however, laid down the conditions that for the management of the Bureau a Committee should be formed representative of all associations of Swiss working-men proportionately to their membership; that the Secretary should be chosen by this Committee and should work under its direction; and that the Department for Commerce should be empowered to send a representative to the Committee's sittings. These conditions were agreed to, and forthwith candidates for the office were invited, the test of fitness being the preparation of the best draft programme of work for the new agency. That of Herr Hermann Greulich, a statistician of repute of Zurich, was accepted, and it was duly submitted to the Government for approval. A congress of labour delegates, representing 142 organisations, 100,000 working-men, and all the cantons, was held in Aargau in April, 1887, under the presidency of the Central President of the Grütliverein, and by this congress Herr Greulich was elected for a term of three years (since twice prolonged) and the definite organisation of the *Sekretariat* was formulated, a work in which Herr A. Scherrer, advocate, of St. Gall, took a prominent part. The new official was by statute made subject to a permanent representative organ of Swiss labour. "For the common representation of the economic interests of the labouring class in Switzerland," ran the first resolution adopted by the congress, "the labour associations of the country form a union known as the Swiss Working-men's Federation." Any and every association devoted to the interests of labour, a majority of whose members were *bonâ fide* Swiss working-men, was to be qualified for affiliation, and all federated associations were to bind themselves to co-operate with the central organisation in all its operations. The "organs" of the Federation were the Swiss Labour Congress (*Arbeitertag*), the "Council of the Federation" (*Bundesvorstand*), the Executive (*Ausschuss*), and the Workmen's Secretary.

To anticipate, the Federation and its sections continue to-day as formed. The Congress meets every three years and is elected by the allied associations, each of which has the right to send one delegate, though his right to vote is dependent upon his representing 250 members, which necessitates the grouping of the smaller associations with a view to the acquisition of voting power. The Council consists of 25 members, chosen by the Congress for a period of three years. They must all be Swiss citizens and at least two-thirds must be working-men. In the constitution of the Council regard has to be had to the due representation of all the languages spoken and the chief industries carried on in the country, and the Council must meet at least once a year. The Executive consists of three members of the Council (and by it elected) resident in the same town or locality (president, actuary, and questor), and it likewise is elected for three years. The Workmen's Secretary is elected by the Congress for the same term. He must be a Swiss citizen, and must work subject to the instructions of the Council, and more especially of the Exeeutive. The statutes of the Federation also provide that the State subsidy shall be applied exclusively to defraying the cost of the Secretary and his work. All other charges—as those connected with the holding of the Congress, and the general administrative costs of the Federation —are defrayed by the federated associations.

The programme which Herr Greulich drew up, and by virtue of which he was elected, placed in the front rank of questions to be advanced by the new agency the introduction of a comprehensive system of industrial accident-insurance, as a preliminary to which the Workmen's Secretary should prepare wages statistics, a return of the benefits conferred by existing sick funds in case of accidents, and an enumeration of the factory and industrial population. The Secretary must, however, further the economic interests of the labour world in general, investigate industrial conditions in all directions, and facilitate the realisation of the needs and desires of the working classes in so far as they were of an economic nature and fell within the rightful province of legislation.

The Federation itself describes the work of the Secretary as " essentially scientific," while upon the Federation rests the duty of disseminating and using the results of his investigations as presented and published from time to time. Neither the Secretary nor the Federation regards public agitation as part of their work : this is left to the affiliated associations and unions. Thus by keeping aloof from agitation they are able to maintain an independent position, to reserve complete freedom of action, and to view questions in broad aspects. Only rarely and on great issues does the Federation pretend to come to the front and make a decisive and open stand, and this is inevitably a weighty step, owing to the immense force which is behind it.

The Workmen's Secretary formally entered upon his functions on June 1, 1887. His first proceeding was to place himself in communication with the various Cantonal Governments of the country, as well as with the Labour Departments of other States, and with private associations concerned with industry, commerce, agriculture, and social reform in Switzerland, between all which and the Secretary there has since been a regular exchange of publications and of views when necessary. The first statistical work undertaken by him was the preparation of an exhaus-

F

tive return of wages paid in the Republic. A good beginning was made; answers were forwarded by a large number of employers all over the country; but these, after all, were found to afford but partial results, and in the absence of means of enforcing information the scheme had temporarily to be abandoned. Better success was achieved in the preparation of statistics of accidents, on which subject two instructive publications were issued in 1890 and 1893 at the request of the Federal Department for Industry and Agriculture. His other publications have included a monograph on the *Institutions of the Paris Municipal Council for the Protection of the Working Classes*, the result of a visit made in 1889; another on Swiss labour movements and strikes since 1860; and papers on the industrial legislation of foreign States, though each annual report concerns itself with a specific phase of the labour question. The Secretary has acted several times on commissions and committees appointed by the Federal Government to investigate matters affecting the interests of the working classes. He is also constantly appealed to for advice by labour organisations and individual working-men, who find in him a convenient intermediary between themselves and the local authorities and the inspectors of the factories, particularly in case of the transgression of the Factory Acts. More than once he has mediated with success in disputes between employers and

employed, and he has on several occasions prepared
statements of the views of the working classes
touching industrial questions pressed upon the
attention of the Federal Government for legislation.

In 1890 an agitation sprang up in French Switzerland for the establishment of an independent Workmen's Secretary for the French-speaking parts of the
country. The special interests of those parts had,
indeed, for some time been in the hands of a French
"adjunct" working in the same office with the
Secretary. The separation desired was happily over-
ruled, and a compromise was come to, and now there
are French agents both at Biel and Lausanne, though
they are subject to the absolute control and direction
of the Workmen's Secretary.

So far, equivocal though the position of the Workmen's Secretary is, in that he is a private and exclusive advocate of the interests of labour in the
pay of the Government—a State-paid agent without
official standing—the relationship has worked harmoniously, and the working classes at any rate have
reason to be satisfied with the arrangement. So,
indeed, the Federal Legislature would appear to be,
for since 1888 the subsidy has increased from £200
to £1000, in view of the really useful national service
which he has rendered. Nor is it likely that either
Legislature or Government will lightly venture to
disturb the understanding now existing. Both know
that at present, at any rate, the institution, irregular

though it may be in principle, is popular with the great mass of the industrial classes, and that the withdrawal of the subsidy would be made a test question at the elections. An official Labour Department may, indeed, be established in time, and the general opinion of those best able to judge is that there is plenty of work for one, for excellent as is the work of the Workmen's Secretary, his influence and usefulness are seriously restricted owing to his entire lack of legal power, but it will exist side by side with the remarkable institution which now holds the field. Said Herr Greulich when plied upon the point, "We have come to stay." And as I saw and conversed with him in his serviceable office in Zurich, surrounded by an international library of social and industrial literature, and with a couple of busy amanuenses at his elbows, he looked like it.

CHAPTER V

THE GRÜTLI ASSOCIATION

THE Grütliverein is the name of the association which has pioneered the cause of labour in Switzerland for over half a century. The oldest organisation of working-men in the Republic, it is also the largest and most powerful, and it may indeed be said to represent to the Swiss factory operative and artisan the idea of solidarity as nothing else does. The Grütliverein dates from a decade which witnessed a great democratic awakening, not only in Switzerland but in other Continental countries. The principal seat of the association has for years been located in Switzerland, and not unfitly so, for East Switzers—the men of Appenzell and Glarus—were its principal founders. The eventful step was taken in 1838 in Geneva, at a meeting of East Swiss friends of labour there resident at the time. At once there rallied to the association men of strong democratic instincts who saw in it a powerful means of leavening Swiss society with the newer ideas of liberty—Professor Albert

Galler, who has been called the intellectual father
of the Grütliverein, Dr. Johann Niederer, teacher
and friend of Pestalozzi, and others, whose names
are held in high honour by the modern democratic
party of Switzerland. These peaceful "conspirators"
called themselves Grütlianer, for said Dr. Niederer:
"I foresee that from this fraternal union of Swiss,
without distinction of cantons, some grand result
may one day spring, as once our free Switzerland
from the Grütli."[1]

The first statutes of the association declared its
purpose to be "free mutual exchange of ideas, enlightenment and instruction in general, and especially
in national affairs," and membership was offered to
any Swiss who had completed his sixteenth year.
Later the statutory purpose was somewhat pedagogic-
ally laid down as "Enlightenment and correction of
views and ideas on simple human circumstances" (I
quote literally), "especially politics, trade, and industry, with particular regard to our fatherland; and
instruction in the simplest and most essential subjects in the sphere of human knowledge."

The association was originally, in fact, very much
what the Berlin Working-men's Education Associations (*Arbeiterbildungsvereine*) were before Ferdinand
Lassalle diverted them into a political channel early

[1] So called from Rütli, the historic meadow in Canton Uri,
where the 33 representatives of the Forest Cantons met in the
night of November 7, 1307, and concluded a pact for the
expulsion of the Austrian bailiffs.

in the sixties: they pursued a distinctly educational and moral mission. It was not long, however, before the association began to take a party character: it became a centre of democratic influence and agitation in a political sense. Thenceforward it expanded more quickly. By the year 1841 branches or sections of the original Geneva association had sprung up in various parts of the country; by 1845 important towns like Lausanne, Berne, Basle, Burgdorf, Lucerne, and Freiburg had opened their doors to it, though in some cases in the face of the active hostility of the police; and during the next decade it acquired by geographical distribution a national character. The members were for the most part young artisans and workmen of strongly progressive ideas on politics and economics, though in general vague enough as to the latter. Yet membership was not confined to the manual working class. Others have always, indeed, been admitted, if not sought, and upon many noted champions of the popular cause, both national and foreign, honorary membership has been conferred. One of the most notable cases was that of Garibaldi, who in 1862 readily accepted the compliment.

Already a political mission was marked as the association's destiny. Radicalism asserted a growing influence within the ranks of the members, especially after the establishment in 1848 of the new Confederation, which had a warm advocate in the Grütlianer, and at last it became openly avowed in the statutes.

During the next few years, however, a complete reaction set in and the Grütliverein suffered as a consequence, like other progressive agencies; the branches in some of the cantons were suppressed and individual members were prosecuted on suspicion of entertaining sympathy with Communistic and Socialistic movements. In Canton Berne especially the hard hand of the reactionary Government fell heavily on the association; the whole of the sections were ordered to dissolve, their books and papers were confiscated wholesale, and such of their members as belonged to other cantons were summarily expelled. This high-handed proceeding of the Berne Government was, indeed, in the end declared by the Federal Executive to be unconstitutional, but two years had passed before the decision was promulgated. When finally the working classes were relieved of all restrictions upon free thought, free combination, and free movement, the association made rapid progress, until at last it covered the whole country as with a network, while its acts and aims more and more brought it as a body into conflict with capitalism as represented by the factory industry and the employing class. That this was a gradual development of the Grütli idea is proved by the fact that at one time questions relating to the merely material circumstances of the members—like that of wages and the conditions of labour—were ruled to be beyond the lawful cognisance of the affiliated sections.

Many a capitalist would be glad if that were the case still. As, however, Marxian propagandism spread in Switzerland, the idea of "emancipation" acquired the upper hand, and to-day the Grütliverein is to all intents and purposes an organisation of Socialist working-men.

Once, indeed, comparatively early in its history, the association had taken practical steps to protect (in its own words) "labour against the pressure of capitalism." This was in 1868 by the contemplated establishment of a loan and savings bank. The initial capital was to have been raised by an entrance fee of one franc, supplemented by a monthly contribution of half-a-franc, imposed on every member of the association. The main object of the bank was to enable members to tide over monetary difficulties and, by advances on liberal terms, to assist the formation of co-operative undertakings. It was, in fact, a weak imitation of Lassalle's working-men's Productive Associations, though here the capital was provided privately instead of by the State. The principle of obligatory payments proved, however, to be unacceptable to the majority, and though the scheme got as far as the raising of over half of the requisite capital, disagreement and want of enthusiasm prevented its full development. While, however, this first collective scheme did not prosper, greater success attended the formation of a sick and death benefit fund, which may be said to have

pushed the bank project—with which it was con-
temporaneous—out of the field. This was established
in 1872 and it exists to-day.

When the Grütliverein eventually resorted to an
unreserved political and social propagandism, it was
under the stress of circumstances. The determining
influence came in 1873, in which year two national
associations were established—the People's Association (*Volksverein*), for the purpose of agitating for
the revision of the federal constitution in a democratic
sense, and the Workers' Federation (*Arbeiterbund*),
whose purpose was "the union of all labour societies
in a federation with a view to an agreement upon
means for the improvement of the workers' lot as a
provisional measure, but ultimately for securing to
them, instead of wages, the full produce of their
labour by means of productive associations, and thus
for the abolition of all class-domination."

Membership of the latter association was offered
to all workpeople resident in Switzerland, whatever
their nationality, and herein it differed from the
Grütli, which only offers membership to Swiss
citizens. Instead of organising resistance to these
rivals the Grütliverein wisely accepted the new
situation which their advent created, and from the
first cultivated close association with both, with a
view to constituting itself a link between their
distinctive yet complementary missions, and this was
done until in time the Grütli committed itself inde-

pendently to wider political and social aims. This
"new course" was manifested most clearly when in
1877 the yearly meeting of delegates adopted by an
overwhelming vote the programme of the Swiss
Social-Democratic Party. Since then the Grütliverein has identified itself more and more with
theoretical Socialism and Communism. Its position
in ordinary party warfare may be described as *intran-
sigeant*. It may always be considered as an energetic opponent by both Liberal and Conservative—
by the former even more than the latter; the
Grütlianer now constitute, indeed, the Independent
Labour Party of Switzerland, and as such they are a
continual thorn in the flesh of orthodox Liberals.

This hostility is clearly avowed in one of the
latest utterances of the association. "Ever more
clearly" (it runs) "is manifested the insuperable
antagonism between the progressive groups. A new
political situation has been created. The forces
which once fought together under the banner of
Democracy have gone asunder. The one, satisfied
with the ideal gains achieved, enjoy in complacent
leisure the fruits of victory won jointly by hard
struggle. The other cannot and will not stop at the
first stage. The goal is not political but social
emancipation. It fights on, under the badge of
Social Democracy, for the emancipation of the working classes from the bonds of economic servitude.
And now the old allies are opposed to each other,—

the one acting as the defenders of capitalism and the despotism of the money-bag, and the other fighting for the emancipation of the proletariat."

However political the association has become in character and aim, the mental improvement of its members is still seriously fostered by many if not all the branches, so that the old idea of the _Bildungsverein_ is still perpetuated. This is done by means of classes in subjects useful to working-men, by lectures, discussions, libraries, reading rooms and reading circles, though singing and gymnastics (_Turnen_) are also cultivated, while among the most important of summer employments are the rural excursions which are arranged for members and their friends. Nor does this exhaust the work of the association. Many of the sections have special funds for helping members travelling in search of work and also the orphans of deceased members.

In principle the Grütli Association has never inquired into or interfered with the religious opinions of its members, religion being regarded as a private matter. Only when the claims of ecclesiastical systems have seemed to come into conflict with the democratic principle of equality before God as before the law—notably in the promulgation of the dogma of papal infallibility—have its responsible leaders broken silence upon the religious question and ventured to warn the members against undue sacerdotal influence. For the rest a Grütlianer may be either Protestant or Catholic, or neither, at will, for the statutes hold no inquisition into his religious convictions.

The association's first organ was the *Nationalzeitung*, but this was not official, and it was not until 1851 that the Central Committee undertook the publication of an official organ in the *Grütlianer*, which originally appeared fortnightly, all members being at first obliged to subscribe. The Central Committee has for many years sat at St. Gall.

A few figures, taken from the report for 1895—a bulky document of nearly a hundred large pages— will attest the influential position of the association to-day. At the end of that year the members numbered 12,700, divided amongst about 350 sections. During the year these sections, besides promoting Labour interests in a variety of ways, arranged 522 political and other discussions and 419 lectures for their members, and provided nearly 7000 lessons in a dozen different subjects. Their libraries comprised over 40,000 volumes. The revenue of 331 reporting sections was £6527, the expenditure £5943, and the accumulated funds were £10,000. The Central Committee met 56 times, attended to the claims and appeals of the sections, issued circulars and leaflets innumerable, and dispensed £175 in help to needy members. Finally, the association's press in Zurich, besides publishing two Labour newspapers—one its own official *Grütlianer*—issued publications to the value of £5300.

CHAPTER VI

MODEL INDUSTRIAL COLONIES

FOR some years a movement in favour of municipal action on the workmen's dwelling question has been spreading in Switzerland, and municipal enterprise in this direction has been emulated by the larger employers of labour. It cannot be said, however, that the housing of the working classes has generally attained to the importance of a problem in Switzerland. It is true that in growing towns like Berne, Basle, and Zurich the rents paid by working-men are frequently very disproportionate to the wages received, and also to the accommodation purchased. For example, an inquiry instituted in the first of these towns a few years ago established the fact that 3450 persons were living in tenements consisting of one room and a kitchen; the dwellings of 1830 persons consisted of a single apartment; while 32,000 persons, or over half the total number affected by the inquiry, lived in dwellings of but three rooms, the average size of which was lamentably inadequate from the hygienic and the moral standpoint equally.

78

Zurich, too, suffers from similar evils. There the rents of small dwellings have become very exorbitant of late years, insomuch that it often happens that working-men have to pay half their earnings, and even more, in rent.

Nevertheless the number of large towns is small in Switzerland, and even in these the strain upon meagre purses is relaxed directly a rackrented tenant removes to the suburbs, which on account of the comparative nearness of his work is seldom difficult. Then, again, the house-industrial system still employs a large portion of the manual-working class, and this system is in the main located in the country or in towns of small size.

The reason which, perhaps, more than any other has led several of the Swiss municipalities and many of the great employers to supply dwellings for the working class is the wholesale removal of old property which has followed in the wake of sanitary improvements and a rage for modern architecture.

BERNE.

The Municipality of Berne has now for some years owned a large number of suburban dwellings, which it built on purchased land for the reception of working-men's families. That the town should have entered upon a project of the kind must be attributed primarily to a serious dearth of industrial

dwellings which made itself felt in the summer of
1889, yet also, if in the second place, to social reform
motives.

It was recognised to be the duty of the community
"to supply the want of cheap and healthy dwellings at all times, so as to relieve the inability of
poor families to find home and lodging because they
had children or because, maybe, the father was ill,
and for the time being was without means, as well
as to prevent the use of mere rooms as dwellings,
often, indeed, overcrowded in the most dangerous
manner; and the dwellings to be provided should,
besides being cleanly and healthy, be allotted a little
garden ground in which families might find beneficial
employment in producing a part of their own food;
while in this way cleanliness and order might be
promoted, and a healthy educational influence be
exerted on the residents."

The foregoing sentences are a paraphrase of the
opinions which found expression in the Town Council
when the project was first mooted, and they admirably describe the policy which has since been
pursued.

The industrial colony at the Wylerfeld, where the
first hundred dwellings were built, is one of the most
interesting sights of the Swiss capital. The site lies
across the Aare, a good half-hour from the centre of
the city, to the north, whither the expansion of
Berne is pressing. A healthier spot could hardly

be found, for the Wylerfeld lies some 1700 feet above the sea-level. The air is of the purest, and if at certain seasons of the year there is more of it than is desirable for old and rheumatically-inclined people, the contrast offered to the close streets and dark, fetid dwellings to which many of the residents were accustomed in the past is highly favourable. At any rate, with an equal birth-rate (36 per 1000 of the population) the death-rate of the Wylerfeld quarter was in 1892 2·5 per 1000 less than the rate for Berne as a whole—17 against 19·5.

The houses are constructed in blocks of two or four, or in rows, and are of wood, though with more solidity and far more pretension than one sees in the ordinary hut of the Alpine village. There are five different types of houses, corresponding to an equal variety of domestic requirement. The smallest houses have a kitchen, a good dwelling- and bedroom, lumber-room and cellaring; and the largest have these apartments, though of wider dimensions, *plus* a second bedroom, the superficial area being thirty and fifty square metres respectively. With very few exceptions the houses stand in spacious gardens, which most of the residents cultivate with taste, skill, and success. Not only so, but near the colony a large tract of land is set apart for allotments, at a very low rate—some 10 francs for 450 square metres —and these afford to a considerable number of men healthy and profitable occupation. Some of the amateur gardeners are able not only to grow all the potatoes and vegetables required at home, but to sell produce to the value of several pounds a year. For the encouragement of allotment cultivation courses of lessons on gardening and exhibitions of produce are held. For juvenile recreation a large playground is provided. The streets are wide and convenient, and are lined with rows of fruit trees, which in time will prove a slight source of public revenue. In the interest of security and providence the municipality sees to the insurance of the house furniture at a low rate, though the colony has special fire-extinguishing apparatus of its own and a volunteer fire brigade has been formed. The preservation of order, the management of the estate, the acceptance and dismissal of tenants (which latter seldom happens), and the monthly collection of rents, fall to a special functionary whose duties are half civil and half police. The responsibility of this official is, however, lightened owing to the fact that each tenant is required to enter into a written contract, binding him to certain reasonable conditions of tenure, as well as to comply with a common *Hausordnung*, which the residents as a rule loyally do. The essential terms of the tenant's contract may be of interest.

"The tenant (×) undertakes to exercise the same care that is shown by an orderly landlord; to be cautious in the use of fire and light; to keep the chimneys, stoves, and hearths scrupulously clean, and to execute slight repairs that may be necessary at his own cost; to carry on no work in the house which may be injurious to the same; and immediately to notify anything about the house which he may regard as defective or dangerous. On the determination of a tenancy the house is to be handed over in as good a condition as when entered; and the tenant is bound at once to make good anything deficient or damaged.] Sub-letting is prohibited without special permission. The provisions of the House Order shall be exactly observed, and the owners reserve the right to inspect the condition of the house from time to time without giving notice beforehand."

The House Order is a more domestic document :—
(1) "All residents have to submit to the directions and regulations of the official charged by the Municipal Finance Department with the special oversight and management of the dwellings, as well as of the overseer of the wells, etc. (2) Every resident is required to conduct himself, both inside and outside his dwelling, in a respectable and peaceable manner. Carousals, and other occasions annoying to neighbours, and the harbouring of persons of bad repute are prohibited. Sub-letting is forbidden save with the special permission of the authorities. (3) In the interest of health the rooms must be cleaned daily and be thoroughly ventilated during the day hours.) The precincts of the house must also be kept in a cleanly condition, and in general everything

must be done which can contribute to the preservation of health, and the prevention of sickness. The keeping of rabbits and hens in the cellars or near the house windows is for this reason forbidden. (4) The drying of clothes in the rooms and under the windows is forbidden. (5) Likewise the cutting of wood in the kitchen and on the entrance stairs. (6) The greatest possible cleanliness shall be observed at the wells, and all unnecessary flow of water shall be prevented. Children especially shall be kept as far as possible from the wells, and for all damage by them their parents will be held responsible. (7) The tenants left and right of the wells shall in turn see to the keeping clean of the space about the same. (8) The washing and drying of linen outside on Sunday is forbidden. (9) Chimneys are cleaned (by the authorities) every three months; delays shall be duly notified. (10) The tenants are finally reminded that the non-fulfilment of the contract of tenancy may entail the cessation of the latter, while those who fulfil their obligations are assured a permanent tenancy."

I entered a number of the houses and conversed with the inhabitants, and it is only fair to the authorities of Berne to say that so far as my observation went their colony at the Wylerfeld is happy and contented. The people pay a very moderate rent, varying from 18 to 26 francs per calendar month (3s. 4d. to 5s. per week), according to the type and

size of the house.   It is safe to say that this rent is
less by 25, 33, and even 50 per cent. than would be
paid in the town for far inferior accommodation, and
the tenants know this and do not fail to value their
privileged position.   One house I visited was tenanted
by an honest-looking tailor in a small way.   His
pride in his home was simply unbounded.   His
garden was a study in colour, the walks were prettily
laid and trimmed, the beds tastefully arranged, and
in one corner there was a small arbour covered by the
clambering foliage of a vine.   The same neatness
and order prevailed within.   The man knew that by
good conduct and punctuality in the discharge of his
obligations he would be able to stay in his house as
long as he liked, and he had taken pains to make it,
both inside and outside, as comfortable as small means
and great energy would allow.   So proud was he,
that he compelled me to enter every room, to spy
into every corner, and finally to climb up the ladder
into the loft.   His rent was about 4s. 6d.

How popular the houses are may be judged from
the fact that changes are extremely rare, and that
there are always far more applications in hand than
can be considered.   Men of good character with large
families are given preference as tenants, as these
have the greatest difficulty in finding good and cheap
housing in the town, and in point of fact, of the
ninety-eight families who resided three years ago at
the Wylerfeld, eleven had seven children each, seven

had eight, four had nine, and one had ten, while the average for the whole was 4·4. I have not dared to ask that these figures might be brought up to date.

But the best remains to be said. Not only does the Municipality lodge some hundreds of inhabitants in these model dwellings, but it is able to make a profit on the transaction. The one hundred houses built at the Wylerfeld cost 457,852 francs, including the land, an average of about £180 each. The rents amount to 27,280 francs yearly, from which have to be deducted land-tax, fire insurance, cost of gas and water, and administrative costs, etc. Yet when these items have been covered there still remains a clear interest of 3·7 per cent. on capital, which is more than the rate at which money can be borrowed. It only remains to be added that the Town Council is now considering the desirability of allowing house-holders to become owners on easy terms of payment. The wise authors of this project will show still greater wisdom if they decide affirmatively.

GENEVA.

The State and Municipality of Geneva are at the present time engaged in carrying out two schemes of working-men's dwellings. Here, too, the effective cause of public action was the inability of the working classes to obtain adequate and healthy lodging, within reasonable distance of their work, at rents in any way proportionate to their wages. In advocating the question in the Grand Council, a Socialist deputy asserted that the modest budget of the average working-man did not allow more than 5s. per week for rent, yet for this he was unable to obtain a dwelling with more than two small rooms besides the kitchen. Three living- and sleeping-rooms were the irreducible minimum of accommodation if the requirements of health and morality were to be observed, and that would mean a rent of at least 7s. 3d. per week, which few working people could pay. The project first proposed was the construction of a large number of cheap and healthy dwellings upon the site of old property in the neighbourhood of the Rue Rousseau, to be demolished for the purpose. One section of the Grand Council was, however, dissatisfied with this scheme, and supported in addition the Socialist proposition for the provision of dwellings on the outskirts, which working-men might be given the opportunity of purchasing within a certain number of years. Both schemes were adopted, though they threatened at one time to be wrecked because of the suspicion of a Socialistic tendency which was alleged against them by the friends of private enterprise.

The first and more ambitious project is expected to involve an expenditure of no less than 2,062,000 francs, or £82,480, for besides some hundred and fifty dwellings it will include a series of arcades and shops on the ground-floor. The buildings will be of four stories, and the dwellings will be of two, three, and four rooms, the area of which will vary from sixteen to nineteen square metres, and each will have separate conveniences, cellar, etc., while wash-houses and drying attics will be used in common. The rents are to be at the rate of 100 francs (£4) per room, the kitchen counting as such, and while it is stipulated that they may be revised every five years, the dwellings are never to forfeit the character of "cheap houses for the working classes." The Municipality is undertaking this large scheme on the strength of an agreement under which the State (Geneva) makes itself responsible for the interest on the necessary loan for a period of thirty years. Thus should the rents of the entire property at any time be insufficient to cover the interest the State will meet the deficit. At the end of this period, in the absence of another agreement, the property is to be placed in the market, and the profit or loss, after repayment of the loans upon it, will be shared equally by the Municipality and the State.

The Socialist scheme is a very different one. For its realisation the Municipality has enlisted the co-operation of the Caisse d'Épargne of Geneva. Interest upon the requisite sum of 150,000 francs (£6000) is guaranteed by the town for a period of thirty years, and with this sum thirty dwellings, each of three or four rooms, with a garden and conveniences,

will be erected in the environs of the city. The
dwellings may be either let or sold at the option
of the Caisse, but preference must be given to existing tenants, who will be Genevan workpeople and
employees, or Swiss workpeople belonging to other
cantons. The rent may not exceed 6 per cent. of
the cost price, including land (an average of £12 a
year), and it will be paid monthly in advance. A
separate account will be kept for each house. To
the credit will be placed the rents paid, and to the
debit $3\frac{1}{2}$ per cent. interest on the price, besides the
costs of repairs, taxes, insurance, water, light, etc.
The balance, if any, will be placed to the credit of
the tenant. At the end of the first year it is open
to the latter to signify his desire to become the
purchaser of his house, in which case a system of
amortisation, which, however, may not be spread
over a longer period than twenty years, is arranged,
though he may pay yearly as much beyond the
annual instalment as he wishes. Should a tenant,
after paying half the price, be unable to continue his
payments, the deed of sale may be cancelled and the
sum he has paid will be returned with interest. In
no case can the Caisse ask more than the net cost
of a house, and in the event of a purchase, all the
sums which may stand to the tenant's credit (as
caused by the excess of rent beyond interest of $3\frac{1}{2}$
per cent., and the yearly costs of repairs, taxes, etc.)
will be deducted from the purchase-money.

Employers of Labour.

Of the model industrial dwellings built by employers those of the well-known chocolate manufacturers, Messrs. Suchard, of Neuchâtel, claim prior mention. Messrs. Suchard have for a long time provided healthy and cheap houses for their employees, either at their own works or in the village of Serrières, near Neuchâtel, and latterly in a model village, founded by the firm on the banks of the lake and named Cité · Suchard. The houses of this new industrial settlement are of two sizes, but otherwise their construction and facilities are identical. They are built in blocks of two houses, each entirely independent of the other. Those of the smaller class contain four living- and bedrooms, also a kitchen, two attics, a vaulted cellar, serving as a workshop, and a wood-house, with the usual conveniences; while those of the larger class contain six living- and bedrooms and the other appurtenances; and both are alike in having a garden. A third type of house has, however, been provided to meet the wishes of a certain number of workpeople, who preferred smaller houses on the flat system. These are built five in a block—two in a story, with three rooms and a kitchen, with a fifth under the gables, each having also a cellar, a wood-house, and attics. There are also common wash-houses, the use of which is allotted by rotation. The rents charged are 17fr. 50c. (14s.)

per month for the small houses and 18fr. 50c. (14s. 10d.) for the larger. This, however, according to Messrs. Suchard's statement, is half their value, and the rents, moreover, include 2fr. 50c. and 3fr. 50c. respectively to cover repairs, which sums are placed to a special account. There is an inspection every three years, and if the house does not require the expenditure upon it of the whole amount which has been accumulated in its repairs fund, the balance is placed to the tenant's savings-bank account. It is contended that this novel system works excellently, inasmuch as it places tenants on their good behaviour, and gives them every inducement to keep their houses in habitable condition. In some cases the tenants have received back the whole of the sums retained from the rents, and in all the rest the half. Messrs. Suchard state that "the gardens are not without influence upon family life, and the husbands take all pains in their cultivation with a view to the production of the best vegetables and the most beautiful fruits." Among the other attractions of the model village is a reading-room, which is open to the men four evenings a week and to the women three, though during the day it is open to both sexes without distinction. Messrs. Suchard give the following as the cost of their industrial dwellings, the land not included:—Blocks of the first class, two small dwellings in each block, £560; blocks of the second class, of two larger dwellings, £640; blocks of the third class, of five dwellings, £1000; while a larger house for the foreman, situated in the centre of the village, has cost £460. It will be seen that the percentage represented by the net rents is small, so that the houses cannot be otherwise regarded than as a meritorious evidence of philanthropic solicitude for the welfare of their tenants.

At Töss, near Winterthur, Messrs. Johann Jacob Rieter and Co., machine builders, have also erected some fifty-five dwellings for their workpeople, and they have provided similar dwellings at St. Gall and Glattfelden. Some stand alone and the rest are in blocks, but in the latter case every family is assured perfect privacy. The accommodation consists of a living-room, two or three bedrooms, a kitchen and a cellar, with wood-house and other necessary conveniences. Each house has a garden, and wash-houses and bathrooms are used in common. The rents for house and garden vary from 208 to 250 francs (£8 6s. 5d. to £10) per year, with an additional 20 francs (16s.) a year for water supplied in the kitchen. The rents are paid fortnightly by deduction from wages, though the water rate is payable every quarter in advance, and if the wages fall below the rent due the balance is payable in cash. The owners undertake to keep in repair the exterior of the houses, and to insure them against fire, to keep the lightning conductors in order, and to maintain the streets, channels, and springs; while the tenant is required

to keep the interior in perfect order and to insure his
furniture. In becoming the tenant of one of the
firm's houses a workman must enter into a formal
contract, which fixes the normal term of notice at
three months on either side, though the firm reserve
the right to remove a tenant in a month should it
have been necessary to discharge him from the works
or should he have rendered himself a nuisance. The
tenant is also required, "in consideration of the
sacrifices which J. J. Rieter and Co. have made in
providing dwellings," to insure himself in a life
insurance company—in an amount which the firm
determine, though the premium must be at least
50 francs (£2)—and the policy must be deposited
with the firm, who see to the yearly payment of the
premiums, which are also deducted from the wages.
Though the reason for insurance is said to be the
provision of a small fund for the workman's family
in case of death, the contract states that the premium
is intended to be of the same amount as the loss
which the firm sustain on the rent charged, and "in
consequence of this the firm require, in the interest
of the families of the tenants, the right of disposing
of these obligatory policies according to the terms of
the contract concluded with the insurance company."
But it is added: "Under certain circumstances
the policy also serves as a bond for rent in arrear, *et
cetera*." Should the tenant wish to increase his
insurance beyond the minimum required by the firm,

he must do so by means of a second or private policy. This insurance provision must be considered in connection with the firm's contract with the insurance company (the *Schweizerische Rentenanstalt, Zürich*). According to this, should a workman leave the service, or cease to be a tenant, of Messrs. Rieter and Co., the latter reserve an unconditional right to continue paying his insurance premiums on their own account, or to cease such payment, in which case the insured sum is proportionally reduced, or to sell the policy back to the insurance company. Private policies are given up to the workpeople, but it rests entirely with the employers to determine whether this is done in case of the obligatory policies or not.

II

INDUSTRIAL PEACE

CHAPTER VII

THE COURTS OF INDUSTRY AT BASLE, BERNE, AND ZURICH

In Switzerland legislation regarding arbitration between employers and employed is left to the cantons individually, and during the last few years a number of them have passed either compulsory or permissive laws on the subject. As a rule, too, the boards and tribunals created to discharge these mediatory functions have done excellent work, though here and there—as was, perhaps, inevitable in so democratic a country—prejudice in the workpeople's favour has been alleged. The only real failure of any moment has occurred in the town of Zurich. On the other hand, the experience of the other three large towns of the Republic—Basle, Berne, and Geneva—has been thoroughly satisfactory.

BASLE.

Industrial Courts of Arbitration (*Gewerbliche Schiedsgerichte*) have now existed in the urban canton of Basle for seven years, and they have thus passed

through the probationary stage. They were established in consonance with a law of April 29, 1889.
This law provides that " disputes in civil law which
arise between the owners of industries and trading
and manufacturing businesses, and the journeymen,
apprentices, *employés*, and labourers employed by
them, concerning the conditions of service, shall be
finally determined by Industrial Courts of Arbitration
in so far as the amount in dispute (exclusive of
interest and costs) does not exceed the sum of 300
francs (£12), and both parties do not demand a
decision by the ordinary civil court." Ten Courts of
Arbitration have been formed for the following groups
of industries and trades :—(1) Textile industry ; (2)
Earth and building works ; (3) Wood work ; (4) Metal
work ; (5) Clothing and trimming ; (6) Food stuffs,
and the liquor trade generally ; (7) Paper industry
and polygraphic industry ; (8) Chemical industry ;
(9) Transport system ; (10) Trade (shops) and other
callings (banks, insurance offices, and employments
connected with literature, art, and science). The
employers and employed of every group choose six
judges each. These are appointed for three years,
but they are always eligible for re-election. Managers
of concerns, if responsible, rank as employers for the
purpose of the law. All male employers and
employed of the age of twenty-four resident in the
canton who come under the law may elect, and are
eligible for election, to the Courts, but no one can

belong to more than one group. A Court of Arbitration is formed of a President (chosen from amongst the Presidents of the Civil Courts) and two of the elected judges, one an employer and the other a workman. The President in every individual case nominates his colleagues from the judges of the group to which the disputing parties belong, having regard always to the nature of the dispute and changing the judges as equally as possible. The disputants must in general appear in person before the Court; only in case of sickness, unavoidable absence from home, or other proved hindrance they may be absolved, and in such event the expense of a deputy cannot be charged to the opposite side. Appeal to the regular courts of law is permitted on questions of competence. In the event of there being raised during the hearing of a case issues which lie beyond the competence of the Court, the latter has, nevertheless, to decide upon the main question, and execution will be deferred until the ordinary civil court has decided upon the other points in dispute. The Courts must meet at an hour in the day which is most convenient to the judges and the disputants; as a fact, the evening is invariably chosen. Sittings are held all the year round as required. The judges are paid the nominal fee of two francs (1s. 8d.) per sitting. No fees are, however, payable to the Courts by either side.

To refer to the recent operations of the Courts, I

find from the official report for 1895 that the judges at the end of that year numbered 102, a reduction of six on the year. There had, however, been an increase in the number of disputes which came before the Courts, principally in the groups for clothing and trimming (five), transport (nine), and retail and miscellaneous trades (ten). The total number of new cases had been 753 (against 504 in the first year, 1890), and five had come from the previous year; 751 cases were adjudicated upon, and seven were carried forward.

It is remarkable that there are comparatively few disputes in the textile industry, though it is the largest industry in the canton. The reason alleged is that the workpeople are able to negotiate through their trade organisations. The groups of industries which furnish most disputes are those of the building trades—whose members are largely Italians, and who, I was assured, are "always quarrelling"—and the food and drink trades, which category comprises the hotels and liquor houses of the town.

I did not find at Basle that that same general satisfaction is felt with the Courts of Arbitration which has been called forth by the *Conseils de Prud'-hommes* at Geneva. The employers have a feeling that the decisions of the Courts in general favour the working classes more than is justifiable. Certainly the labour party have a decided advantage in regard to the constitution of the Courts. Their leaders are careful to get on the Courts wherever possible, and no chance is lost, so far as they are concerned, when disputes have to be decided, of furthering the labour side. On the other hand, it is held that there is a tendency for employing members of the Courts, or certain of them, to vote with the labour side from motives of trade rivalry or with the object of ingratiating themselves—a delusive and futile species of opportunism, no doubt—with the working classes. It is estimated that the Courts are applicable to some 21,000 workpeople of both sexes, of whom scarcely a third are eligible to elect or be elected to the Courts.

BERNE.

Courts of Industry (*Gewerbegerichte*), charged with the duty of conciliating industrial disputants or deciding between their claims where conciliation is impossible, have been in operation in Berne since the beginning of 1895. They may be said to have been established by the express wish of employers and employed equally. No sooner had the Cantonal Decree of February 1, 1894, upon the organisation and procedure of these Courts been published, than the Municipal Council issued inquiries to all the commercial and labour organisations of the city, as well as to private representatives of the principal industries, asking their opinion as to the local need of such a method of preventing dissension between

capital and labour. Not only was there no objection
to the establishment of Courts of Industry, but without a single exception the replies urged the Council
to lose no time in calling them into existence. Thus
encouraged, President Müller and his colleagues at
once formulated a scheme suited to the peculiar
circumstances of Berne, and after being duly endorsed
by a vote of the citizens (2985 for, against 179 to the
contrary), it came into operation on January 1, 1895.
For the purpose of Courts of Industry the trades and
occupations of the city have been divided into eight
groups : (1) Group for food stuffs and the chemical
industry ; (2) Clothing and dress; (3) Textile
industry ; (4) Metal working; (5) Wood manufactures and furniture trade ; (6) Earth works and
building trades; (7) Graphic industries ; and (8)
Merchandise, transport, and conveyance. For each
of these groups 16 referees or assessors (*Beisitzer*)
have to be elected triennially, consisting half of
employers and half of employed, all of course belonging to the trades concerned, and chosen by their
peers. The number can, however, be increased to
eighteen or twenty if the Municipal Council should
be advised that this is desirable. An assessor is
disqualified from serving if he fails to follow his
calling a whole year, if he passes from the position
of employer to that of workman, or *vice versâ*, and if
he ceases to possess the requisites of eligibility ; also,
if he permanently removes from the district, and if

ho is guilty of improper conduct. When the members of a Court are reduced by any reason to one-fourth, by-elections to fill the vacancies are necessary. The assessors in turn elect (in plenary sitting) a President (*Obmann*) and two deputies, who may not be either employers or workmen. In addition, there is a General Secretary, whose salary may range from £40 to £80, as the Municipal Council may from time to time determine. The President conducts the sittings of the various Courts and also all plenary sittings, but in the event of two or more Courts sitting together his deputies share the work. It is the duty of the General Secretary to receive applications for the services of the Courts and to take the necessary steps to give effect to them, as well as to see to the promulgation of all decisions. The members of a Court are paid for each sitting—the President and deputies five francs (4s.) and the assessors three francs (2s. 5d.). The municipal police are charged with the preparation of the voting lists for the various groups and the carrying out of the elections.

The competence of the Courts is thus defined : " For the pacific settlement of disputes which arise out of contracts affecting apprenticeship, service or work in the domain of manufacture or handicraft, between manufacturers and master artisans on the one side and their workpeople, journeymen, *employés*, or apprentices on the other side, Courts of Industry

may be established. Where conciliation is impossible,
these have also to decide without appeal all disputes
the value of which does not exceed 400 francs (£16)."
Where the sum in dispute is £4 and under the
Court consists of only three members—the President,
an employer, and a workman ; but for larger sums
of five—the President, two employers, and two workmen.   Sittings are public except during attempts at
conciliation.

The right of appeal within three days is allowed in
the following cases : (1) When the sitting at which
judgment was pronounced was not made known to
the appellant and he did not attend ; (2) when the
Court was not legally constituted ; (3) when the
appellant was refused a legitimate hearing; (4) when
the unsuccessful party was not capable of conducting
his case and had no representative ; and (5) when
more was awarded to the successful party than was
claimed.   Should the appeal be found reasonable the
case is sent again to the Court, but before new judges.
It is also provided that a case can be reopened by
the defeated party if it can be shown, within one year
from the award, that new and material evidence has
come to light.

So far the Berne Courts have been able to hold
the balance fairly evenly between the two sides, and
though they cannot be said to have yet left the
experimental stage, both employers and employed
desire their continuance.

ZURICH.

In 1889 a system of Courts of Arbitration combined with a Board of Conciliation was established by private agreement amongst employers and employed in Zurich, and though it was dissolved "until further notice" in 1891 it is rather of more than less interest on that account, since it seems to offer an illustration of the disadvantages under which an institution of this kind labours when the status and prestige which come from association with public authorities are lacking.

Six associations of master craftsmen and six of journeymen belonging to the same crafts combined to form a Union for the purpose of submitting contingent disputes to the process either of arbitration or conciliation in accordance with the nature of the issue. The associations were the following :—

	Members.		Members.
Master Joiners' Association	40	Journeymen Joiners' Association	130
„ Stonehewers' „	12	Journeymen Stonehewers' Association	150
„ Masons' „	30	Journeymen Masons' Association	100
„ Cabinetm'k'rs' „	75	Journeymen Cabinetmakers' Association	180
„ Tinners' „	30	Journeymen Tinners' Association	50
„ Painters' „	30	Journeymen Painters' Association	50
Total	217	Total	660

The statutes of the Union merit notice, for though the machinery of arbitration is at present standing it may at any time be put in motion again.

The Courts of Arbitration were made competent to decide wages disputes, while the Board of Conciliation was to "adjust or settle" disputes on issues arising out of contracts of service—"for example, labour regulations, the payment of wages, the term of notice, the apprenticeship system, and other matters to be mutually agreed upon."

The affiliated associations undertook that their members should resort to the Courts of Arbitration in the event of disputes and to abide by the decisions given, while they bound themselves similarly to submit to the Board of Conciliation all matters which fell within its jurisdiction. An executive was formed of two representatives of every affiliated association (one being in each case chosen by the employers and the other by the employees), all being men practically engaged in the trade which they represented, and this body, together with a President [1] elected triennially by itself, yet being neither employer nor employee, was charged with the general oversight of the institution.

Separate Courts of Arbitration were formed for all the six trades represented in the Union. For this

[1] Herr Oberrichter G. Müller was the later President of the Executive, and to him my thanks are due for information here given.

purpose the masters' and journeymen's associations each elected three arbitrators and an umpire (with a deputy). A Court was formed of two arbitrators— one for each side—and an umpire, who was in turn the masters' and the men's nominee. Legal representation was prohibited, and only in the event of "absolute hindrance" might the absent party be represented by a fellow employer or a fellow workman as the case might be. As a rule arbitration proceedings—which were conducted publicly and were gratuitous from beginning to end—were confined to disputes not exceeding 500 francs (£20), and disputes involving larger amounts and claims arising out of employers' liability were only considered on the written undertaking of both sides to abide by the decision, and in such cases two arbitrators were called in on each side instead of one.

The Board of Conciliation consisted of the entire executive of the Union. On cases for conciliation being reported to the President he called the plenary Board together and invited each of the parties to send three representatives to debate the matters in dispute before the same. Should an agreement not ensue as the result, the Board sent a deputation to the meetings of the disputants charged with a conciliatory mission, and in the event of failure the Board was again summoned, this time without the representatives of the masters' and workmen's associations for the trade affected, and a decision was promulgated, to which both parties were bound to submit.

The necessary funds were raised by levy upon the members of all the associations. It was provided also that an association might withdraw from the Union at the close of a calendar year by giving three months' notice.

For the first year, the Union worked well and harmoniously, though it is noteworthy that not a single employer submitted a case to either Court or Board. Several incidents combined to bring about the dissolution. A bad effect was created amongst the master craftsmen by the appearance before the Court-room on one occasion of a band of workmen, friends of a disputant, who assailed the employer in the case with groans and other expressions of disfavour; while on another occasion an employer on returning home alone late at night from a sitting in which he was concerned was followed by workmen who threatened violence. Incidents of this kind were symptomatic of the hostile and arrogant spirit in which a section of the working classes sought the services of the Courts, and this spirit provoked first apathy and then discontent on the part of the employers' associations, which were probably glad enough to withdraw directly a valid excuse offered itself. This was found in a decision of the Board of Conciliation of January 31, 1891, in a case in which certain cabinetmakers made application (1) for the fixing of a minimum wage of 45 centimes ($4\frac{1}{2}d.$) per hour, with 33 per cent. more for overtime and Sunday work; (2) the abolition of a Labour Bureau which had been founded by the Master Cabinetmakers' Association (seeing that the men had machinery of their own); (3) the maintenance of a normal work-day of ten hours; and (4) the regulation of piece work. The Board virtually decided in the men's favour on all points save No. 3, and the decision caused much dissatisfaction in the employers' circles. The Association of Master Cabinetmakers withdrew, and the other masters' associations soon followed suit. In general it was found, indeed, that the pacific objects of the Board of Conciliation were difficult of realisation. Where there was any question of either employers or employed giving way and surrendering any of their rights (legitimate or assumed) great obstinacy appeared on each side, and no people were more uncompromising than the smaller employers, who refused to be "dictated to," and resented any pretensions on the part of their men.

The place of the Courts of Arbitration and the Board of Conciliation has not yet been occupied by any similar machinery, and industrial disputes, in so far as the civil law is competent to deal with them, have had to be submitted to the ordinary tribunals. The Municipal Council of Zurich has, indeed, issued a decree intended to discourage strikes, by offering to take the initiative in conciliatory measures in the event of disputes occurring, but it has in general been ignored.

CHAPTER VIII

THE CONSEILS DE PRUD'HOMMES OF GENEVA

THE position of the canton of Geneva is unique, inasmuch as the French system of *Conseils de Prud'-hommes* has been adopted. These *Conseils* were established in 1883 in accordance with a law passed at the instigation, in the first instance, of a number of industrial organisations of the canton. Originally, the disputes to which they referred were those arising in industry and commerce only; but in 1889 the law was extended, and it now provides that "disputes which arise between masters and workmen, employers and employed, employers and apprentices, masters and domestic servants, in all that concerns the payment of services, the execution of work, and the contract of apprenticeship, are judged by the Tribunals of *Prud'hommes*."

The *prud'hommes* are chosen in equal numbers by the employers and employed, acting separately in groups of industries—so many *prud'hommes* for each group—but only persons of Swiss nationality, in the possession of full political rights, can elect or be elected. The managers and directors of companies are regarded as employers. There are two main classes of *Conseils* —(1) Those relating to manufactures and commerce, and (2) those relating to agriculture and private individuals. Each *Conseil* consists of thirty members, fifteen being employers and fifteen employed, regard being had to all the species of employment represented as far as possible. Election is for two years, but retiring *prud'hommes* are eligible for election. Election is by *scrutin de liste*, ballot, and relative majority; the ordinary day of election is the first Sunday in October; and the poll is open for six hours, from nine o'clock in the morning. When deaths or retirements diminish the membership of a *Conseil* by a fifth part within more than six months of the ordinary elections, the Council of State must order by-elections. Ineligibility ensues when a *prud'homme* ceases to follow his calling for one year, when he changes from employer to workman, or *vice versâ*, and when he becomes insolvent. The members of a *Conseil* take the same oath of office before the Grand Council as do judges. Each *Conseil* elects by ballot a committee, consisting of a president, a vice-president, a secretary, and a vice-secretary. The presidency falls alternately to the employers' and employees' half of the *Conseil*, and the balance is preserved by the provision that if the president be an employer the vice-president must be a workman, and *vice versâ*. The same

arrangement applies to the secretaryship and the
vice-secretaryship. Each *Conseil* is divided into the
following sections: (1) Board of Conciliation (*Bureau
de Conciliation*); (2) the Tribunal proper; (3) the
Chamber of Appeal (*Chambre d'Appel*); and (4) a
committee for supervising apprenticeships and the
sanitary arrangements of workshops. For the avoid-
ance of friction, and the securing of complete independence, it is provided that upon none of these
bodies can an employer and one of his workpeople,
or otherwise a master and his servant, sit together.

To particularise: (1) The Board of Conciliation is
composed of an employer and a workman, who pre-
side in turn, beginning with the elder. Where conciliation fails in cases involving sums not exceeding
twenty francs (16s.), the Board constitutes itself a
court of summary jurisdiction, and pronounces final
decision, against which there is no appeal. In the
event of disagreement, or of the Board lacking the
necessary material upon which to come to a decision,
the case passes on to the Tribunal. The sittings of
the Board, except those in a legal capacity, are
private.

(2) The *Tribunal de Prud'hommes*. Cases which
are not determined by the Board of Conciliation
come before this second division of the *Conseil*, which
is composed of a president, three employers, and three
workpeople. The first two conduct the proceedings
in turn. Witnesses are heard on both sides, and

I

experts may be called when necessary, these being women where the occupations in respect of which dispute has arisen are followed exclusively, or almost so, by their sex. Final decision is given in cases involving sums not exceeding 500 francs (£20).

(3) In disputes involving a larger sum, the case may be carried forward to the Chamber of Appeal within five days. This body is composed of a president, a secretary (without deliberative voice), five employers, and five workpeople, none of whom may have taken part in earlier proceedings regarding the case under deliberation. Otherwise the same provisions apply as to the *Tribunals de Prud'hommes*.

(4) There is also the institution of the Mixed Court (*Cour mixte*). It is provided that the Tribunals dealing with a dispute regarding which an objection on the score of competence or pendency has been raised should, as a first step, determine upon this objection. Such decisions are, however, subject to an appeal, whatever the sum in dispute, before the *Chambre d'Appel*. The parties may apply to be heard against the award, so far as relates only to competency and pendency, before a Mixed Court, composed every year of two Judges of the Court of Justice (nominated by the latter) and three *prud'hommes*, chosen from and by the *Chambres d'Appel*. The awards of this Mixed Court are final, subject to the prerogatives of the Federal Tribunal.

As to general provisions. The sittings of the

Tribunal de Prud'hommes and of the *Chambre d'Appel*
are public, and take place in the evening in places
appointed by the Council of State. A *prud'homme*
may be challenged—(1) should he have a personal
interest in the dispute at issue; (2) should he be the
father of, or be otherwise related to, one of the
parties up to the degree (inclusive) of cousin-
german; (3) should there have been a criminal
action between him and one of the parties or relatives of the same : (4) should a civil action be then
pending between him and one of the parties or
relatives; and (5) if he has given advice in the
matter.   A fee of three francs (2*s*. 5*d*.) per sitting is
paid to each *prud'homme*, but the presidents and
secretaries receive two francs (1*s*. 8*d*.) more, and a
prud'homme regularly convened who fails to attend
without legitimate reason may be fined as much as
twenty francs (16*s*.).

The *Conseils* have, however, other functions of a
useful kind.   They may be called together to deliberate upon questions interesting to national industry
and commerce at the instance of the Council of
State, the Grand Council, or a majority of presidents
and vice-presidents of all the groups, and on such
occasions the *doyen* of the presidents is called to the
chair.

Another important department of their work is
that relating to apprenticeship contracts, whose due
execution is the concern of a Special Committee.   In

the event of friction the case in question is laid before the *Conseil* concerned, which advises in the matter, and, if necessary, sends it on to the Tribunal. This same Committee superintends the sanitary conditions of places of service and the salubrity of raw material. The Committee is composed of four employers or masters, and four workpeople, or other *employés*—all, of course, *prud'hommes*.

There is, furthermore, a Central Committee of the *Conseil* composed of two delegates (an employer or master, and a workman or other *employé*) chosen from the Special Supervisory Committees of the different groups, and elected by the same for two years. This Central Committee mediates between the *Conseils* and the Council of State and its different Departments, and to the Council of State it presents a report yearly upon the work of the *Conseils*. It also exercises general supervision over the different groups of *Conseils*, and sees to the execution of the law in general. The Committee may at the request of a group appoint special committees, composed of members of the groups or of persons not belonging to the *Conseils* at all, for the study of questions interesting to national industry and commerce. It may also institute investigations into the hygiene of the places of service and the healthiness of raw material. The results of such inquiries are laid before the Council of State, and the Committee sees to the execution of the hygienic measures which that

body orders. It also superintends the technical
education of apprentices.

That the *Conseils* have justified their existence,
and established themselves in public estimation, is
attested by the fact that while on the first reference
to the popular vote on October 29, 1882, the law on
the subject was only accepted by a majority of 839
votes (5550 to 4711), the majority in its favour at
the *plébiscite*, on the occasion of the revision in 1888,
was 2256. It is not too much to say that the hopes
of the promoters of the *Conseils* have been altogether
realised. Far from having fostered ill-feeling, and
provoked disputes between employers and employed,
they have made industrial relationships more ami-
cable, have removed many misunderstandings and
defects in relation thereto, and have promoted the
formation of organisations on both sides for the
friendly readjustment and regulation of the conditions of labour.

As proving the efficiency of the *Conseils*, and the
confidence felt in them by the public, it may be
stated that since the law came into force there have
only been thirty-nine appeals to the Court of Final
Instance, the Federal Court of Law—thirty by the
employers and nine by the workpeople. In twenty-
five cases the judgment awarded was confirmed, in
three it was modified, in six quashed, and in five
the Court proved to be incompetent. Disputes are,
indeed, submitted to the Courts, both by employers

and employed, very readily, and complete success and permanency can be claimed for this satisfactory manner of promoting industrial peace in Geneva. Not a few Swiss municipalities have benefited by the ripe experience of Geneva, and various foreign Governments have found her *Conseils* worthy of special study.

CHAPTER IX

SOCIETIES OF PUBLIC UTILITY

In most cantons of Switzerland there exist societies
of very comprehensive aims, and uniting the best
activities of the public-spirited and benevolent of
both sexes, whose title may be rendered "Societies
of Public Utility" (*Gemeinnützige Gesellschaften* or
Gesellschaften des Gemeinnützigen). There is a distinctly eighteenth-century sound about such a name
as this, and indeed some of the societies date from
over a hundred years ago. That of Berne is the
oldest and was established in 1759.

It is difficult to define the position of the societies
exactly, for in the sphere of social welfare they profess
to recognise no limitation of their influence and usefulness. They seek, in fact, to discharge the multi-
plicity of philanthropic duties incumbent upon
modern society which are everybody's business in
general yet somehow nobody's business in particular.
The Society of Public Utility is a sort of philanthropic clearing-house, by whose agency the human
objects of educational and reformative experiment

are handed over to the experts most interested in, and best able to deal with, their case. For as a rule a society is made up of many sections, each charged with specific work and doing it. That of Berne, for example, has affiliated with it some seventy sections, having an aggregate membership of over 9000.

Not only are there cantonal societies, but these are supplemented by district and urban societies working on the same lines, whilst acting as a bond between all is a society for the whole Confederation, whose seat is in Zurich.

One of the best of the urban societies is that of Basle—the "Society for Promoting the Commonweal," as its title may be rendered (*Gesellschaft für Beförderung des Guten und Gemeinnützigen*). It was established in 1777, and has now a membership of over 1000 persons, of whom a large portion are both workers and givers. When founded the society for a time pursued benevolent purposes somewhat indiscriminately. It was not long, however, before it promoted systematic movements in the interest of thrift and education, and these have multiplied in variety and number until now it either supports entirely, or liberally subsidises, over fifty institutions and agencies for the welfare of the industrial and the poorer classes of Basle. Of late years some of the society's functions have in part been transferred to public bodies—the Town Council, the Poor-Law Authority, the Churches, and the like—for they were

undertaken at a time when social reform was less
regarded as a concern of the organs of local government than it is in these days. Nevertheless, the society
still occupies ground which neither legislation, nor
religion, nor yet private enterprise is likely for a long
time to dispute, and the good work which it achieves
from year to year is simply incalculable. The
ordinary revenue is about £4300, though this is
variously supplemented, thanks to the plan which
is followed of securing the help of other organisations, public and private, whenever the society thinks
that it is doing their work and promoting their aims.

Here only the briefest possible outline of the
society's work can be given. Its first agencies were
educational, and education continues to play a prominent part in its operations, albeit in this sphere the
society finds itself contracting rather than extending
its scope owing to the advance which is being made
year by year by the State and Municipality upon
the province hitherto held by private and philanthropic enterprise. Its oldest institution is a school
for languages, in which French, Italian, and English
are taught to some 800 or more young men and
women. Its object is to offer to young people of
small means, which do not allow of private study,
the opportunity of making some acquaintance with
modern tongues, especially from the commercial side,
without any cost at all. For the most part the
pupils are apprentices of both sexes, shop assistants,

and clerks. In summer the classes are held before seven o'clock in the morning, in winter in the evening. In this behalf the society spends some £200 yearly. The society also carries on schools for children of very tender age. It has 14 schools of this kind, conducted in convenient centres of the town, and as a rule there are from 50 to 60 in each, in charge of a school-mistress. Their total maintenance costs £700 a year, a third of which comes back in fees, and in addition it subsidises nine others. The total attendance exceeds 1400. (The society carries on eight Sunday Schools; it has a series of sewing, tailoring, and mending schools for schoolgirls; certain of the lady members teach schools wherein factory women and girls are similarly instructed; and there are finally schools for women generally, with courses of instruction every winter in systematic domestic economy.)

In the same sphere of work the society organises winter lectures for the people, with singing classes, besides supporting a permanent music school, and there is a special section for the dissemination of wholesome literature, which manages to employ in this useful way over £1000 a year. Libraries are maintained for the working classes, for citizens generally, and for youths, in various parts of the town, and for their use nominal fees are charged. The first of these contains over 4000 volumes, and had in 1894 750 readers of both sexes; the second

contains over 6000 volumes; while of youths'
libraries, which are open to the children of the
schools, there are several. The yearly expenditure
on all is £170, of which the society pays nearly £100.
There are eleven other small People's Libraries
(*Volksbibliotheken*) for indiscriminate use in different
quarters of the town, having altogether 8000
volumes, and over 1500 readers. The Natural
History Museum, the Historical Museum, and the
Industrial Museum also receive important help from
the society.

There is a special committee of the society whose
duty it is to interest itself in, and to promote by
practical measures, the welfare of the factory population (the *Commission für Fabrikarbeiterverhältnisse*).
It manages sick, old age, burial, and other benefit
funds to the number of nineteen, with an annual
revenue of some £4100. This is independent of the
society's "Death and Old Age Fund" (*Sterbe- und
Alterscasse*). The number of insured in the first
department of this fund was, in 1894, 2238, for an
aggregate amount of £104,000, and in the latter 103,
maturing pensions of £1100 on the whole. The
combined invested capital exceeds £100,000. Re-
verting to the Factory Committee, it also awards a
number of annual premiums of 40 francs (£1 12s.)
to respectable male operatives, artisans, and men-
servants who have worked the longest time under
the fewest number of employers, just as another

department of the society does for domestic servants; and it carries on free cookery schools for the wives and daughters of working-men. The society promotes home industry by the lending out of sewing, silk-winding, and knitting machines, which may be acquired at cost price by their users on easy terms of payment.

Better still, it is the administrator of a number of model working-men's dwellings, situated within the confines of the town. For this enterprise, which was for evident reasons placed on a company basis, a capital of £2400 was raised, this being, however, supplemented by loans of £5520 on mortgage. The tenements have, as a rule, three rooms besides a kitchen and other necessary accommodation, and the rents vary from 260 francs to 340 francs (£10 8s. to £13 12s.) a year, which allows of a dividend on shares of 3½ per cent. after provision for amortisation and a reserve fund.

Other institutions for the especial benefit of the working classes are reading-rooms and a people's eating-house, where about 100,000 meals are sold a year at prices within the reach of light purses.

Excellent work is done in encouraging thrift by means of savings banks, which date from 1810, and whose depositors exceed 30,000, with an invested capital of nearly a million pounds sterling, on which interest of three per cent. has hitherto been paid, though it is not believed that this rate can be continued much longer. The depositors are for the most part artisans, factory operatives, shop employees, small public officials, labourers, and children, the last forming a large percentage. To this department of the society's work belongs a pawnbroking establishment (*Pfandleihanstalt*) and loan office, which offers to the needy temporary relief on easier conditions than can be obtained at private agencies of the kind. Legally the loan-office is entitled to charge interest of two per cent. monthly, on advances up to 50 francs (£2), and one per cent. on large amounts; but the monthly rates charged are: On loans not exceeding 50 francs, 1½ per cent.; from 50 to 500 francs, one per cent. : 500 to 1000 francs, three-quarters per cent.; and over 1000 francs, half per cent.

To the domain of philanthropy proper belong substantial contributions to the maintenance of an orphanage, homes for deaf and dumb children, and homes for waifs and strays, and to the "Asylum for the Aged," which is carried on in the Basle Hospital, and in which a dozen pensioners—all of whom have qualified for admission by long residence in the town —enjoy home and careful nursing.

The miscellaneous philanthropies include a boot and shoe fund, a fund for clothing poor scholars (3000 of whom benefit in this way in a year, at a cost to the society of £1000), soup kitchens, and an agency for lending out gratuitously surgical and other instruments required in sickness. Here, too, may be named the support during the term of their indentures of deserving apprentices whose parents have not an excess of means. The amounts granted vary from £4 to £12 a year, and take the form either of the payment of board, the payment of apprentice-ship premiums, or the purchase of tools, etc. The recipients number as a rule from 30 to 40.

One other side of the society's work must be referred to, and it is not the least important. It is the recreative. A well-equipped gymnasium is kept for the use of athletic associations, both private and in connection with schools and societies. Swimming and bathing establishments are maintained in the Rhine, and they are used by some thousands of persons of both sexes and all ages yearly. Moreover, a Children's Game Committee exists, with the object of organising evening amusements for the young, both out of doors and indoors, according to the season, while another committee holds "pleasant Sunday evenings" in winter for the children of the very poor, who are assembled in convenient halls and entertained with pictures, music, and stories. The society even goes so far as to provide skating facilities during the frosty season in various quarters of the town for adults and children separately.

The wonder is that the Basle Commonweal Society is able to do so much with resources so modest.

An excellent example of an urban society working

within a smaller sphere is that of St. Gall. One of the most useful works which it has of late undertaken is the reformation of the Poor Law system so far as regards the treatment of children, whom it desires to see entirely removed from the workhouses, and trained in separate homes or in private families. Its efforts are also felt to advantage in the encouragement and support of deserving apprentices and in the maintenance of reading-rooms for the people.

III

THE PROBLEM OF THE UNEMPLOYED

K

CHAPTER X

Two defects have long been advanced against the English Workhouse system—not that its defects are hereby exhausted. One is its failure, in all but the most exceptional cases, to distinguish sufficiently between the *bonâ fide* industrial traveller and the mere loafer, who likes his loaf well enough, but will not work for it save under compulsion. The other is the inadequacy and futility of the Workhouse labour-test, inasmuch as it is penal and in no sense educative, whereas the idle need more to be trained to love of work than to be punished for scorning it. Both these defects are covered in some degree by institutions peculiar to Germany and Switzerland— the first by the Natural Relief Stations, the second by the Labour Colony.

Originated in Germany, the Relief Stations (known generally as *Nationalverpflegungsstationen*) now cover as with a network not only that country, but also Switzerland, and in general they are conducted under the auspices of the local administrative

131

authorities, though there are many exceptions. In
the industrial life of both countries they fill a most
important place, and in England, where the honest
but empty-pocketed wayfarer has no choice between
the Workhouse and the police-station—unless he
should beg his lodging-fee—they deserve to be better
known. A considerable section of every industrial
community is continually in motion. This fluent
population may be divided into two main categories.
There is the vagrant class—the shiftless nomads of
the lower strata of society, the idlers, the vagabonds
and rogues, all of whom live more or less by mendicity
and mendacity ; but there is also the smaller and
decenter class of unwilling unemployed, whose idleness is often more their misfortune than their fault,
and who are compelled to roam from town to town
in search of work. To these two principal divisions
of unsettled labour may be added a large number of
respectable artisans who are induced to travel by
curiosity, restlessness, or a desire to widen their
technical knowledge and experience—men, for the
most part still young, who act on the principle of
Goethe's saying, that

> " To give one room to travel is it
> That the world was made so large."

It is to meet the needs of the industrious portion
of this roaming population that the Relief Stations
have been established. Virtually the ground is not

touched by any other agency. The trade guilds do, indeed, do something to relieve the temporary want of unemployed members, and to provide them with funds for travelling in search of work. But the resources of the guilds are generally very limited; moreover, neither in Germany nor Switzerland does their membership represent any great proportion of the working classes. Here the Relief Station comes in and does a beneficent work. Its object is to offer to workmen "on the road" something of the comfort and the security of home, and any one acquainted with the private lodging-houses—facetiously called "model" houses—which exist in our towns for the accommodation of sojourners of the poorer class, will appreciate their purpose and acknowledge their usefulness. Here the young apprentice (*Bursche*) fresh from home, and entering on his *Wanderjahre*, or the journeyman (*Geselle*) seeking settled work, is sure of pleasant quarters, respectable company, a healthy atmosphere (both physically and morally), and all this at no cost.

In both countries national unions exist for the purpose of securing uniformity of regulations and relief, and though the institutions of Germany are admirable, those of some of the cantons of Switzerland are understood to take the palm in regard to efficiency and success. Eleven of the German-speaking cantons of Switzerland are united in an "Intercantonal Union for Relief-in-Kind." They are: St.

Gall, with 10 stations; Thurgau, with 15; Zurich, with 50; Glarus, with 6; Schaffhausen, with 4; Lucerne, with 24; Berne, with 47; Aargau, with 18; Soleure, with 5; Urban Basle, with 9; and Appenzell, a.R. In six of these cantons the system is organised completely on State lines, and in the rest it remains in private hands, though the public funds are largely laid under tribute. In these 11 cantons no fewer than 162,910 tickets were issued in the year 1895, of which 45,466 were for dinners only, and 117,444 for supper and lodging. Fifty-eight per cent. of the whole recipients were Swiss, and the rest were mostly Germans and Austrians. The cost exceeded £5200, but half of which was borne by the Cantonal Governments, while the balance came from district funds. The average cost of dinners alone was 3d., and of supper and lodging 8d.

Combined with the Relief Stations there are frequently to be found Labour Registries. Here is kept a register of the chief employers of labour in the locality, and of the works which may at the time be in progress, with vacancies which may have been notified, and an attempt is made to find work for such of the callers as have no definite prospects before them. No charge is made. Thus during 1895 the Relief Stations of the Swiss cantons referred to supplied work in no fewer than 2426 cases.

The regulations of the Zurich Stations may be instanced as good examples of the general rule.

According to these an itinerant workman desiring
free lodging for the night is required first to have
his papers "controlled," which is done in many cases
at the police-station, though the inspectors are
mostly civic officers or private individuals. The
examination satisfactory, he receives a stamped and
dated certificate entitling him to admittance to the
lodging-house ; his name, calling, age, and home
being entered in a register for record and future
reference. Not only is he lodged, but an attempt is
made to find him work in connection with a register
of employers which is kept on the premises, and new
garments may be given to him if he should stand in
need. As a rule, no relief is given if the applicant
proves not to have been in work for three months
and if he refuses work offered to him, though
exceptions are frequently made. A workman is only
given dinner or lodging once in six months at the
same Station. When the wanderer goes on his way
he takes with him a stamped and dated certificate,
which he must present at the next place at which he
stops, but he must have travelled at least two hours
from one Station to another in order to qualify again
for relief. The mid-day meal given consists of soup,
vegetables, and bread ; and supper and breakfast consist of coffee (or soup) and bread. No brandy may
be served to a caller. In case of disorder of any kind
the offender is at once handed over to the police. In
some places there are special homes, known as

Herbergen; in others the workmen are quartered
in approved houses, and in others, again, in respectable inns, though the last-named mode is generally
allowed to be objectionable, and only in cases of
necessity is it resorted to. As a rule the walking
distance from one Station to another is from six to
ten miles.

A few figures will show on how large a scale this
system is established in the canton of Zurich—with
a population of over 300,000—where it is conducted
on official lines at public cost.   The canton is divided
into 12 administrative districts, which have on an
average four Relief Stations each.   During the year
1894—the last for which I have been able to obtain
a complete report—77,620 certificates were issued,
of which 55,883 were for supper with lodging, and
21,737 for dinner. About 60 per cent. of the persons
relieved were Swiss and the rest mostly Germans
and Austrians.   The cost for the year was about
£1100, nearly all of which came direct from the
cantonal exchequer.

Far from encouraging vagabondage it is the
experience of the canton of Zurich that the Relief
Station system, thanks to the stringent control
which is exercised, has a contrary effect.   The
genuine seeker after work knows that he can claim
accommodation free, while the idle vagabond knows
that his non-possession of a travelling warrant
inferentially proclaims him to be a pest whose proper

place is the Workhouse (which in Germany and
Switzerland is something very different from our
institution of the same name), and he makes himself
as scarce as he can.

On the whole the authorities both in Germany and
Switzerland are thoroughly satisfied with the Relief
Station system, which is an incalculable boon to the
working classes and by them is heartily appreciated.
At present a determined attempt is being made to
supersede private enterprise, where it still exists, by
public organisation and administration, and this is
the inevitable goal of the system in both countries.
It is obvious that only when the Stations altogether
pass into the care of the administrative authorities
will it be possible to secure that uniformity of management which is so desirable. It is also probable that
more will be done to bring the Stations into closer
relationship with the various trade organisations, so
establishing a heartier co-operation between the
two. Each may be regarded as complementary to
the other, though it has not hitherto been possible
to bring them sufficiently close together. When
this is done the influence of both will be enhanced,
with unquestionable benefit to the working classes.

One serious defect, or rather deficiency, of the
official Relief Stations must be pointed out. There
are no Stations for the reception of women. The
lack has been much debated, yet at the same time
it has been held, rightly or wrongly, that to make

special provision of the kind might tend to foster
itinerancy amongst single women, and discourage
those settled habits which in workers of both sexes
are desirable.

It remains to speak of specific municipal action in
this same sphere of social reform. In some of the
larger towns homes for travelling workmen have
been established on quite a large scale. Berne is
especially well off in this respect, for it possesses
several institutions of the sort. The best is known
as the " Passers' House " (*Passantenhaus*), which is
carried on in connection with the Burgspital, and
offers free food and lodging to decent persons of
both sexes. The only credential asked for is written
evidence that the applicants are genuine out-of-works
who are desirous of finding employment, and people
of the most various character enjoy the hospitality
offered within its walls. While I waited a few
minutes in the call-room to inspect the sort of wayfarers who sought food and shelter here, there entered
three travel-worn yet honest-looking working-men.
One was an Alsatian, who presented a Relief Travelling Ticket (*Unterstützungswanderschein*), signed by
a clergyman ; another a sharp-eyed young *Bursche*, of
18 or 19 years who produced his Labour Book ; and
the third was an Italian, who was admitted on the
strength of his passport. It rests with the Master of
the house to decide whether an applicant should be
rejected on account of uncleanliness or any other

reason; and in this event he is directed to the police authorities, who find him other free quarters. Admitted within the doors the wanderer is given clean, if simple, lodging, with wholesome food (soup and bread) evening and morning, and again at noon, should he stay so long. Not only so, but if his clothes are worn he may hope to receive new ones when he proceeds on his journey; if his pocket is empty, he may be given a few shillings to see him through the next day or two; and in case of sickness he is handed over to the hospital quarters, where he receives the best attendance and nursing which are at the command of a richly-endowed foundation. The condition is, however, imposed that no person may seek admission more than twice in the same month, or more than thrice in the same year. This institution supplies a great social need and does a noble work. By its instrumentality no fewer than 17,000 persons—a third of them foreigners—men for the most part, are helped in their search for employment every year, and of these some 300, as a rule, receive new shoes.

Most of the institutions of which I have spoken are more than mere free lodging-houses; for they have their religious, educational, and social sides as well. The directors and superintendents, too, are more than landlords; they are friends and advisers, to whom the sojourner can resort in confidence, certain of receiving the best possible help. The

homes are not, indeed, temperance houses according
to the English idea, but while light beer is generally
provided spirits are excluded, and the common
incidents of public-house life—card-playing, billiards,
and boisterous song—are not tolerated. They are
simply quiet and decorous houses of call, where
wandering toilers rest and are thankful for the
kindly care, the thoughtful foresight, and the paternal
solicitude which minister to their well-being. With
these "homes from home" to resort to, the respectable workman may make the entire circuit of the
country, if needful, under conditions that do not
militate against his morality and self-respect. He
is given the opportunity of keeping out of the current
of promiscuous humanity—composed of elements so
largely degraded, baneful, and turbulent—which is
expressed by the pregnant word "trampdom," and
the perils of such an association are well known to all
social reformers.

The Roman Catholics of Switzerland also work on
the same lines, though their agencies are intended
especially for their co-religionists, in connection with
the Catholic Artisans' Association (*Katholischer Gesel-
lenverein*), whose seat is in Cologne. In most towns of
importance provision is made under the auspices of
this powerful guild for the housing of Catholic working-men, both resident and itinerant, and in ten of
the twenty-eight places in which branches exist the
association has homes of its own—Zurich, Lucerne,

Winterthur, Altstätten, Appenzell, Gossau, Rappen-
will, Rorschach, St. Gall, and Utznach.   The association was founded in 1846 by Adolf Kolping, a priest
of Cologne Cathedral.   Its avowed object is to
encourage and help artisans of Catholic persuasion
to the cultivation of " a strong religious and civic
sense and life, in order to the development of a
capable and honourable master-class," and the means
employed in the pursuit of this excellent end are—
public lectures, classes for ordinary instruction (as a
rule the three R's, drawing, geography, history, and
natural history), song, the reading of suitable literature, and mutual stimulus generally, as well as
mutual assistance in time of need.   Membership is
offered to any unmarried Catholic journeyman
between the ages of 15 and 26 who lives or desires to
live a regular life, though Protestants are admitted
in exceptional cases.   The fees are small—a few
pence a month—in return for which all the educational, social, and religious advantages of the association and its homes are offered to members, together
with, at death, free burial with full fraternal honours.
The house (*Vereinshaus*) at Zurich is a large, handsome, and well-equipped building, where over 200
persons can be permanently lodged, while accommodation is also reserved for a number of casual wayfarers.
The latter only pay the ordinary membership fee of
7*d*. per month.   Permanent residents have separate
quarters, for which the sum of from 7 to 12 francs

(5*s*. 7*d*. to 9*s*. 7*d*.) is charged monthly, exclusive of board.   In winter educational classes and recreative gatherings are periodically held, and the institution acts as a week-day rendezvous for the Catholic working classes of the town.

CHAPTER XI

THE Labour Colony is an institution of German
origin. The story of its inception may be told in a
few words. The first colony was established by
Pastor von Bodelschwingh in 1882 near Bielefeld, in
Westphalia. It was a product of economic factors
peculiar to that time. Partly owing to new legislation enacting for all Germany free choice of
occupations, but also owing in no small degree to
the change from hand to machine power, which was
revolutionising a large number of industries, and
destroying others, there sprang up throughout the
country, and especially in the industrial districts, an
exceptionally large number of unemployed. It has
been estimated that no fewer than 200,000 persons
were wandering upon the highways of Germany
at that time in search of work. Bielefeld, being
situated on the great highway from Cologne to Berlin,
had more than its share of penurious visitors, and
before he founded a colony for the employment of
surplus labour, Pastor von Bodelschwingh did much

to cope with an incessant claim upon the philanthropic resources of the town. Believing charity,
however, to be an objectionable substitute for honest
work, he purchased a farm, with buildings, a few
miles out of Bielefeld, with the object of working it
with the labour of the wayfarers, who had hitherto
thrown themselves on the poor-rates and on charity.
In the purchase of this farm—which, with later
additions, approximates 1000 acres—Pastor von
Bodelschwingh received both public and private
financial help. The estate was a compact tract
of sandy land of small value until reclaimed by
dint of a great expenditure of labour. Placing
at the head of the colony an experienced farmer,
trained in his own ideas, Dr. von Bodelschwingh
practically opened its gates to all the unemployed
who passed that way, the only condition of entrance
being adhesion to the regulations of the establishment. Thus was founded the first of a large series
of colonies which have together done much to
alleviate, though not by any means solve, the
problem of the unemployed in Germany. Before
two years had passed colonies had been formed in
eleven parts of Germany, and the total number is
now nearly thirty, while the movement has spread
to other countries—Switzerland among them. As
to Germany, well-nigh 100,000 men have been received into its various settlements, there to be
trained in habits of industry, sobriety, and self-

respect; and a very large number have passed out
to fill paid positions. At the same time a per-
ceptible influence has been exerted upon vagabondage
and mendicity, and to this extent public order and
private philanthropy have benefited. It is not too
much to claim, too, that the colonies, in thus maintaining in wholesome restraint and occupation so
numerous a highway class, have proved a great
deterrent to crime.

To sum up, the mission of the Labour Colonies is
industrial and religious. They offer the unemployed
not money but work, and that work is associated
with a moral discipline of a helpful and elevating
character. Among Silesian enthusiasts in the cause
the story is told of how a dilapidated vagabond
passed a colony in that part of Prussia, and observing
the motto over the door, "Ora et Labora," knocked
and asked for "Mr. Ora." But it was "Mr. Labora,"
the vigilant director, who answered the call, and no
sooner had the explanation been given, than the
beggar expeditiously went his way. This is not
only history, but parable.

The Tannenhof Workmen's Home (*Arbeiterheim*)
is the older and more important of the two colonies
established on Swiss soil. Though it owes its origin
and support to the canton of Berne, it is located in
the canton of Neuchâtel. The colony lies at
Witzwyl, several miles from the capital of the canton,
and is planted on a tract of flat land, arid enough

when first settled—land over which a plough had
never passed—but now passing fertile in parts, and
everywhere vastly the better for the cultivation it has
received during the last seven years.   Where then
there were moorland and peat-pit, there are now
cornfields, vegetable gardens, and a well-kept grazing
farm, and if the desert has not exactly blossomed as
the rose, it has become a place of prosperity and
rejoicing.

The estate consists of forty hectares of land, a
patch of woodland, two houses, and farm buildings.
In its original state it was purchased for some 60,000
francs (£2400), to which must be added about half
as much again for farm stock, live and dead, new
buildings, and general equipment.   Although largely
supported by public funds, the colony was organised
and is still managed by private citzens, the first
mover in the matter being Lieutenant-Colonel Jean
von Wattenwyl, of Berne.   By his instrumentality
the *Verein Arbeiterheim* was formed; an association of thirty members, himself the president, the
qualification for membership being the purchase of
at least one share (*Antheilsschein*) of 100 francs (£4).
To the capital several parishes and a number of corporations contributed, and the balance was subscribed
by philanthropic persons.   These all, together with
the canton of Berne and a few churches, continue
regular supporters of the colony from year to
year.

In the words of its statute, it is the object of the *Verein Arbeiterheim* to "offer temporary home, by the carrying on of a farm, to unemployed men seeking work, and to discharged convicts of the Berne penitentiaries, where in return for shelter, food, and wages they will be required to do agricultural work until they find permanent occupation elsewhere." Yet entrance is by no means restricted to such applicants; in general all comers are welcomed, especially in summer, when land labour is plentiful and labourers are few. The majority of the colonists, indeed, are procured by much the same method that sends applicants for help to the offices of the Charity Organisation Societies. A destitute man begs bread or alms at the door of a member of the association; instead of receiving what he wants, a ticket for the Labour Colony is offered him, and he is invited to better his fortunes there. This ticket is a severe test of the genuineness of the common beggar's profession that he has no work to do, and—unkindest cut of all—cannot find any. The number of knocks at the door of the Tannenhof Home is quite out of proportion to the number of directions thither bestowed by the members. Many are called, few chosen. It is the old story. Not a few destitute persons, of course, find their way to the colony without the advice of members—owing their knowledge of it, maybe, to comrades on the road, to the self-effacing

policeman, or to common report—but in the main
the colony is fed by its own friends.

Each colonist on admission is required at once to
enter into a written contract to remain at least two
months, and to do his best at the work to which he
may be put, in return for which he receives food,
shelter, and body-linen, with medical attendance in
case of sickness. Should the master or Father
(*Hausvater*) be pleased with his work, he may be
awarded a bonus to the extent of fifty centimes per
day. The accumulated bonus is paid to him when
he leaves the colony, less deductions for clothes,
tobacco, and similar extras, for clothing may be
obtained on request and be paid off by industry.
As a rule, indeed, the director endeavours to prevail
upon the colonists to remain until they have earned
a new outfit and the tools of their trade, so that
they may be in a better position to find work on
discharge.

The daily routine is decidedly rigid. The very
"order of the day" indicates that the Home contemplates serious business. As its supporters say:
"At the Tannenhof the precept 'He who will not
work shall not eat' is followed. He who is willing
to work, however, receives work and also food,
clothing, and shelter, and not least a Christian home,
with divine service and homely admonition on a
Sunday by clergymen friendly disposed to the
Home." At 4 a.m. in summer—that is, from May

to October—and at 5 a.m. in winter (though at 3 a.m. in hay and harvest time), all the colonists are awakened by bell. Beds are made, ablutions performed, and then follows short prayer, after which work at once begins. At 6 in summer and 7 in winter comes breakfast. At 9 there is a ten minutes' pause for the hurried eating of a piece of bread. The dinner-hour is 12, and from 12.30 to 1 there is a rest. Work is then resumed till 4, when a ten minutes' pause is allowed for vesper-bread, followed by work till 7 or 8. Supper and prayers succeed, and then comes bed. On Sunday the inmates rise later, at 6, and retire earlier—at 7.30. The dietary, let me say in passing, is plain but ample. Bread *ad libitum* may be eaten at every meal; there are two vegetables at dinner all the year round, with nutritious soup; and twice a week (Thursday and Sunday) there is fresh meat.

At the time of my visit, in July, land work was in full swing, and the colonists were in the field twelve or fourteen hours a day. They seemed a contented lot of men. The utmost order and harmony prevailed both indoors and out. Every one knew his task and followed it without word of direction. At noon the sun-burnt band assembled at the large *Speisesaal* for dinner. It was homely fare, but there was no stint—soup, steaming potatoes, cabbage, salad, bread, and a tin of milk for each. The Father —an honest-looking, somewhat naïve and evidently

thoroughly practical peasant from the Emmenthal,—
home of world-renowned cheese—sat at the head
of the table and shared the common repast. The
meal, like all others, was introduced with prayer,
and it ended with a short Bible reading. The
appetite satisfied, plates and mugs were cleared
away by one of the colonists, and the family broke
up, each going his own way during the short time
allowed at midday for relaxation. The family idea
and relationship struck me forcibly throughout.

While agriculture thus keeps most of the colonists
busy in summer, the less robust, and the physically
defective, are set to tailoring and shoe-making, and
yet others sell peat and wood in the town of
Neuchâtel and elsewhere.

The home produce of the colony is not insignificant. The value for 1895 was as follows:—hay and
grass, 3450 francs; rye and spelt, 1500 francs;
winter and summer wheat, 1660 francs; oats, 1261
francs; potatoes, 2320 francs; turnips, 697 francs;
beet-root, 584 francs; and milk (27,438 litres), 3292
francs, a total value of nearly £600.

All the joinery and smith's work needed on the
colony are also done at home; so is the bakery; the
pig-stalls and poultry-yards help the commissariat
in a measure, while the wool clip keeps a large part
of the settlers in good stout stockings.

So far the average number of colonists in residence
has been about 35, the extremes being 50 (when no

further applicants can be accommodated) and 18 or
20. The colony is busiest in winter. The rush
begins about November, when harvest is over, when
casual work declines with the year, and when, too,
the highways are less congenial by day, and the hay-
stacks and woods by night, than in summer-time.
The migratory habits of the colonists are, indeed,
very prejudicial to the commercial success of the
undertaking. During three months of a recent
summer the manager found himself left with but
eleven colonists, and these, he laments, "were of
little use for agriculture—two cobblers, a tailor, a
basket-maker, two joiners, a mason, a milker, a
carter, a young man who still had to learn to work,
and a man with a wooden leg." Where adequate
farm labour has thus been lacking, paid labour has
had to be called in, to the terror of the treasurer.
So, too, it happens that the colony has the largest
family when there is the least work to do. Hitherto,
there have always been more applications for admission in winter than could be entertained, and
even those admitted have in large part simply been
consumers without contributing materially or at all
to the productivity of the colony. It is hoped,
however, to remedy this evil by the introduction
of simple handicrafts, and already, indeed, basket-
making, straw-plaiting, and sundry wood-working
are attempted on a small scale.

The colony does not pay its way, nor have its

friends ever expected it to do. If the association
were to restrict the admission of colonists at all
seasons to the minimum number absolutely requisite
to the carrying on of the farm and gardens, it would
probably be possible to place it on a paying footing.
But this would be to restrict and indeed to defeat
the main objects of the Home, which is intended to
be a training-ground where able-bodied men may
be introduced to agricultural work, and thus be dis-
couraged from crowding into the towns, there to
swell the army of the workless, the homeless, and
the discontented. If, however, the friends of the
colony have some 6000 francs (£240) to raise yearly
somehow, in order to make the balance-sheet square,
it would be rash to say that the money so expended
is thrown away. Apart from the moral influence
exerted by the colony upon its workers, its operations
materially relieve the poor funds of surrounding
parishes.

It can hardly be said, however, that the ideals of
the *Verein Arbeiterheim* have so far been quite
realised. The colony has in the main attracted a low
class of inmates. Roughs, loafers, and idle fellows
who merely wanted to tide over an inhospitable
winter in comfortable quarters have formed its
principal patrons. Of the 54 colonists admitted
during the year ending March 31, 1894, 25 had
been convicted, and the punishments which have
to be inflicted, the dismissals from the colony, and

the close check which has to be kept upon the movements of the lawless testify to the rough material with which the energetic and tactful *Hausvater* has to deal. This official, whose reports betray a pretty talent for characterisation, describing the 50 men who formed his by no means happy family early last year, speaks of them as including "young and old, from 18 years to the fifties, the halt and the sound, some hungry, and all thirsty, the half-naked and the fairly-clothed, gross criminals and slight, industrious and lazy, straightforward and hypocrites and rogues. And, indeed, there were worm-eaten pieces in them all." Only once, however, has the Father had to call in the services of the police. It was the case of a gaolbird who had been thirty times convicted; he smuggled a quantity of brandy into the home, and lively scenes followed in the night hours.

But there are better as well as worse, and it is pleasing to read that discharged colonists frequently visit their old haunts on Sundays and holidays, to inquire how the colony is faring and to scrutinise their successors and their achievements.

While thus a good work has undoubtedly been done and a good influence exerted, on the whole the hopes of the philanthropists who form the *Verein Arbeiterheim*, and who started the "Arbeiter-heim Tannenhof," are directed to the future.

That the colony will long continue to be located

at Tannenhof is uncertain, since the existence of a
penal settlement in the neighbourhood has given
rise to apprehension lest an undesirable contact
between the inmates of the two institutions might
be developed.   The promoters are therefore in
negotiation for the removal of the colony to another
estate, which besides, from its uncultivated condition,
would provide ample pioneer work for a long time
to come.

CHAPTER XII

BERNE.

THE Municipality of Berne established a Labour Bureau (*Anstalt für Arbeitsnachweis*) in 1888, and it has since been carried on with signal success. The Bureau is divided into two main departments—one for industry and trade in general, and one for domestic and hotel service. The latter has from the first done an important work, and the Bureau appears to be more popular, alike amongst mistresses and maids, than private servants' registries and agencies, one reason being the high fees generally charged by the latter. The average daily number of applicants of all kinds is about ten in summer, and twenty in winter. The fees charged at present are given in the table on the following page; at the time of my visit, however, they were being revised with a view to a reduction.

Should work not be found for the applicant the registration fee is, of course, alone payable. Double fees are charged for non-residents of Berne, but no

155

	Registration fee. Centimes.	On arranging work. Centimes.
Outdoor labourers, masons, and domestic servants and inn employees	10	20
Where wages exceed 20 francs (16s.) monthly	40	40
Where wages do not exceed 20 francs (16s.) monthly	30	30
Artisans { journeymen.............	30	50
Artisans { masters	50	50
Apprentices ....·..........	50	50
Clerks, shop employees, etc. ...	80	80

fees at all are asked of the very poor. The Bureau was originally managed by a committee of eleven members as follows : three by the Municipal Council; four by the Artisans' and Industrial Association (*Handwerker und Gewerbeverein*) of Berne ; two by the Berne branch of the Grütli Association ; and two by the General Working-men's Association of Berne.

By a recent revision of the statutes, however, the management has been placed on a new basis, and the committee is now composed of nine members, three chosen by the employers, three by workpeople, and three by the Municipal Council, election being for four years. This committee also has charge of the Municipal Unemployment Insurance Fund, to which reference will be made later. The director of the Bureau is appointed by the Municipal Council at the nomination of the committee, and holds office

by terms of three years.   His salary has hitherto
ranged between £120 and £160.   The Municipality
provides the Bureau with furnished offices, bears the
cost of requisite books and stationery, heating and
lighting, and also meets deficits between expenditure
and the moderate revenue from fees, which deficit
is usually about £130.

The Bureau is by its constitution compelled to
keep aloof from industrial disputes.   In the event of
any occurring it ceases for the time being to enroll
either employers or workpeople affected.   As will be
expected the Bureau always has a far larger number
of applications for work than for workers in the
general labour department, yet during the last year
for which a report was issued, employment was found
for just half of the seekers, while three-quarters of
the offers of work received from employers could be
met.   In the domestic servants' branch, on the other
hand, there were as many offers of positions as
demands for them.   There was no very great variation in the number of applications from season to
season, as appears from the following figures for the
men's department :—January 31, February 16, March
36, April 42, May 38, June 31, July 30, August 54,
September 36, October 35, November 25, December
22; total 396.   The greater number of applications
came from unskilled and outdoor workmen of various
kinds.   The women's department told the same tale.
The figures for the same year were :—January 95,

February 100, March 124, April 124, May 102, June
90, July 81, August 115, September 111, October
103, November 88, December 52; total 1185. Here
almost half of the applications came from general
servants (524), next followed cooks (129), and next
charwomen (111).

The Municipality of Berne has not, however, a
monopoly of labour registration in the city. A
number of private agencies also exist—some older
and others formed since the Labour Bureau began,
the most noteworthy being those in connection with
trade organisations.

BASLE.

The town of Basle has had a Labour Bureau since
the summer of 1890. It was organised and continues
to be supported by the Grand Council of the Urban
Canton, which furnishes the requisite rooms and
both subsidises the Bureau and is responsible for
deficits upon each year's working. The board of
management consists of eleven nominees of the
Executive Council, three being employers and three
workpeople, while the female department of the
Bureau is subject to the oversight of a ladies' committee of six members, one of whom should attend
at the offices daily. There are also two paid managers
—one for each department. In the event of a strike
it is open to the Executive Council to suspend opera-

tions either altogether or for the industry affected until a settlement has been arrived at. The Bureau is open from eight to twelve and from two to five on week-days, except Saturday, when it closes at noon.

The Bureau has worked remarkably well, and nowhere has the fee system met with success. The State subvention the first year was £145 12s., but it has since fallen as low as £24, the great bulk of the expenditure being covered by the fees, which have reached as much as £200 in a year. They are fixed as follows—

	Employers' fees.	Employees' fees.
Outdoor labourers, factory operatives, and day workers of both sexes	40c.	20c.
Artisans, both journeymen and apprentices........................	60c.	30c.
Domestic and inn servants, and shop employees.................	1 fr.	50c.

In the case of foreigners (who are chiefly Germans) the fees are doubled. Applicants for work who offer themselves on a recommendation from the poor-law authorities, private agencies for the relief of the poor, or the clergy, are registered gratuitously. The payment of a yearly subscription of ten francs entitles the giver to use the Bureau *ad libitum.*

The Bureau is used readily by employers and employees of all industries and trades, but here as everywhere unskilled labourers are the most numerous seekers of work in the men's department. Farmers and farm-labourers, however, form a large contingent of patrons. Such is the confidence enjoyed by the Bureau among housewives and domestic servants, that private employment agencies have been largely superseded.

St. Gall.

Here the Municipality and the local Commonweal Society (*Gemeinnützige Gesellschaft*) have combined to establish a Labour Bureau, but it has not been a great success, for the workpeople's associations have never taken to it kindly. The Town Council undertakes to pay a subsidy not exceeding £80 a year, and in addition fees are levied of fifty centimes and one franc upon native and foreign applicants respectively, half being returned in the event of work not being found.

CHAPTER XIII

AT Geneva the institution generally known as the Labour Exchange (*Chambre du Travail* or *Bourse du Travail* as it is known in France) has been adopted. The law on the subject is dated October 19, 1895, so that the agency has only well got into operation, on which account it is only possible to state the lines which it is intended to follow. This law empowered the Council of State to employ the sum of £400 in "facilitating the organisation by the working classes of a Labour Exchange for the use of workpeople resident in the canton of Geneva." Future grants were left to be determined by circumstances, but the entire cost of the Exchange will be a communal charge.

The objects of the Exchange are thus set forth in the statutes: "To bring the demand for and the supply of work as speedily as possible together, to facilitate the meeting together of working people in a building of their own for the discussion of their general interests, for collecting statistics for the

purpose of demonstrating whether there be a dispro-
portion between work and workers, and conducting
all the researches necessary to acquainting working
people and *employés* generally of both sexes with
outlets for their activity both in Switzerland and
other countries."

Besides acting as a Labour Bureau the Exchange
will instruct parents in matters relating to apprenticeship, and help them in choosing for their children
such employments as may seem to offer the best
prospects of regular work.   It will also help working
people in the case of accidents, and advise them upon
the laws relating to employers' liability, factories, and
wages contracts.   No fee whatever can be required
in return for such help and advice.

The full control of the affairs of the Exchange is
vested in the hands of an "administrative committee,"
which is responsible for the proper and orderly
working of the Exchange, and the right use of its
finances.   It must render an account yearly to the
Council of State.

This committee consists of eleven members (who
must be of Swiss nationality, and resident in the
canton, and at least seven Genevans) elected by
the judges of the eleven groups of the *Conseils de
Prud'hommes*, one by each group.   The committee
chooses an executive from its midst, consisting of a
president, vice-president, treasurer, secretary, and vice-
secretary, election being for one year, with the chance

of re-election. The meetings of the full committee are held at least once a month, and of the executive once a fortnight. Members of the committee receive a fee of three francs (2s. 5d.) per monthly sitting, and the president, vice-president, and secretary two francs (1s. 7d.) additional. A committee-man failing to be present at three consecutive meetings forfeits office, and the Council of State must order his replacement.

The principal official is, of course, the secretary. It is his business, besides attending to the correspondence and the ordinary routine work of the Exchange, to receive and register offers of work and requests for the same, which are to be displayed in a conspicuous place in the building. He is expected to keep in touch with the labour market both of Geneva and of the neighbouring towns, so as to be able to direct inquirers for employment to likely quarters. Every week he must also send to the Press a report containing the returns of the labour registry and other facts of interest to the working classes.

As to the prospects of the Labour Exchange of Geneva, I am unable to say more than that it stands well with the working classes, to whom, indeed—or more properly to their representatives in the Grand Council of the canton—its establishment is due. The project may be said to have originated with the Socialist faction of that assembly, but the other parties—Conservative, Radical, and Catholic—took favourably to it, and it passed without difficulty. The Labour party certainly had a strong argument in the fact that the Cantonal Government has long given a considerable subvention to the Chamber of Commerce,[1] an institution which promotes the special interests of manufacturers and merchants just as the Labour Exchange will now promote those of industry.

[1] The State subsidising of Chambers of Commerce is no rare thing in Switzerland.   In return the Governments do not hesitate to call in the assistance of these bodies when it can be done with advantage to the public interest.   The report of the Department for Commerce and Industry of the Genevan Council of State for 1895 refers to this matter as follows : "The Chamber of Commerce, owing to the means of investigation in its possession, and its constant contact with our commercial and industrial population, is a useful auxiliary to the Department for the provision of information and data of which we stand in need."

CHAPTER XIV

OUT-OF-WORK INSURANCE

IT has fallen to Switzerland to make the first practical experiments in compulsory out-of-work insurance. A species of insurance against the material consequences of deprivation of employment is effected in England, in a more or less intentional way, by many of the voluntary trade organisations which have taken root here as in no other country in Europe. Owing in some measure to the failure of Swiss Trade Unionism to realise the larger aims which are both recognised and achieved in the land of their origin, and also to a remarkable development of State Socialism, some of the Cantonal and Municipal Governments of Switzerland are endeavouring to compass the same end by the aid of legislative measures. Voluntary insurance against worklessness has for several years been operative in the town of Berne; the town of Basle purposes shortly to introduce an obligatory system; but in St. Gall an experiment with compulsion has already been made. The variety of these three systems of insurance, and the profound interest of the subject, will justify an account of each separately.

Voluntary Insurance at Berne.

The Berne institution merits preferential notice, inasmuch as it is the first established in Switzerland under municipal auspices, though the efforts of the Town Council were, to some extent, anticipated by the local labour party. Here insurance is entirely voluntary. The bold venture of Berne was undertaken with a view to coping with certain thorny facts of poor-law and philanthropic experience, and was no mere light-hearted excursion into the tempting domain of political experiment. The scheme owes its inception, in fact, to the failure, or at least the insufficiency, of the ordinary existing agencies for the relief of distress caused by scarcity of employment amongst the labouring population in the winter months of recent years. The unemployed problem bore with great stress upon this town during the winter of 1891-92, which was so long and severe as to necessitate public relief and private benevolence upon an extraordinary scale. At that time Dr. Wassilieff, the secretary of the associated labour organisations of Berne, instituted a careful census of the unemployed, and the immediate result was the formation of a committee of citizens charged with the duty of relief, for which purpose a public fund was raised. This committee soon found that the widespread worklessness to meet which it had been called into existence was in reality no isolated incident, though it happened then to have taken an aggravated form. Before the winter was over the conviction had been formed that as the regularly-recurring distress from lack of work in the winter months, far from diminishing, showed every sign of increasing, private charity, in endeavouring to relieve it, was essaying a task quite beyond its power, even if not beyond its legitimate scope. Experience had already shown that the continual and deepening drain upon civic benevolence thus caused tended to curtail the help of which ordinary charitable agencies and movements stood in need. Not only so, but it was recognised that the system of relief was itself open to serious objection. The thriftless were encouraged to neglect the duty of laying by against the inevitable rainy day, inasmuch as there was a certain prospect that a tender-hearted community, more regardful of their welfare than they were themselves, would step in at the critical moment and protect them, and those dependent upon them, from the result of their own wanton improvidence. But almost worse still, the absence of organised co-operative provision against loss of work placed the deserving unemployed under the frequent and painful necessity of becoming paupers and receivers of doles.

During the succeeding spring and summer a

systematic investigation of the question of unemployment, its causes, and the alleviation of its consequences, was conducted by the same committee, whose eighteen members included men well qualified to undertake such work—University professors, town councillors, journalists, and labour leaders. One of the recommendations drawn up as a result of this investigation was the organisation by the municipality of a voluntary system of out-of-work insurance. Before anything was done, however, by the municipality, Dr. Wassilieff had himself set on foot a partial system of insurance—applying only to unskilled labourers, of whom over 600 voluntarily joined before the winter of 1892-93 was over. This was done by means of a Labourers' Federation (*Handlangerbund*), whose statutes stated :—

"The Federation aims at providing work for unemployed members, and work offered by the management may not be declined. Relief is only paid in cases of absolute unemployment. Unemployment resulting from accident, sickness, and bad weather alone entitles to relief, while such as is a consequence of idleness and notorious intemperance will be punished by the forfeit of relief for as long a period as three weeks."

Part of Dr. Wassilieff's scheme was an agitation for an increase of wages of five to ten centimes (½*d.* to 1*d.*) per day, which increase was intended to be used for insurance against sickness and worklessness.

His insurance fund did undoubted good, but it was soon recognised to be inadequate, since it expressly excluded large sections of the labouring class which, like the unskilled labourers, were subject to intermittent employment. The committee pressed the question strongly and repeatedly on the Municipal Council, by whom it was sympathetically received, for early in 1893 the resolution to establish, under municipal auspices and with municipal help, a comprehensive system of insurance against worklessness was formally adopted.

The existing statutes, as revised after two years' experiment, date from the beginning of 1895. According to these, "Every working-man (*Arbeiter*) sojourning or settled in the parish of Berne can join the insurance fund. Admission is effected by announcement to his employer or to the president of his trade union or direct to the director of the fund." The funds which are used in unemployed relief are drawn from four sources: (1) Contributions of the members; (2) contributions of the employers; (3) a municipal subsidy; and (4) private gifts. The contribution of the insured is fixed at fifty centimes (about 5*d.*) monthly all round, payable regularly at the end of the month, and payment is made by means of "insurance stamps" which are attached to the book of membership. The municipal subsidy is for the present fixed at 7000 francs (£280) per year, though originally 5000 francs (£200), and it is noteworthy that employers' and other voluntary gifts realised half as much as the subsidy the first year, but an equal amount the second. Should there be a surplus on any one year it is carried forward, but in the event of a deficit the fund must get out of its difficulties without further call upon the foster parent, the municipality.

Those members who have paid their contributions regularly are entitled, in the event of worklessness, during the months of December, January, and February only, to claim benefit from the fund for a maximum period of two months during the same winter. No relief is, however, paid for the first week of worklessness, and it is stipulated that members shall have been insured for six months before they can fall upon the funds. Benefit is paid weekly. For the first 30 days of worklessness the maximum allowance is paid—1.50 franc (1s. 3d.) to independent, unmarried members, and two francs (1s. 7d.) to married members and such as have others dependent on them; and the payments for the second month are regulated by the Board of Control according to the state of the exchequer. The date at which relief ceases altogether is also determined by the Board on the merits of each individual case. As a guarantee of good faith every person in receipt of benefit is expected to show himself twice a day, at such times and places as may be appointed. The reservation is also laid down that "the resources of the insurance fund may not be

employed in the relief of members whose worklessness is the result of idleness, disorderly conduct,
quarrelsomeness, disobedience, and misdemeanour of
any such kind, or who have refused work without
adequate reason, nor may they be employed for the
support of strikers."

Both the Labour Bureau and the Insurance Fund
of Berne are under the control of one committee
as well as under the superintendence of one paid
official. The committee is composed of nine members
—three elected by the employers, three by the workpeople, and three by the Municipal Council, election
being for three years. The members elect a president
and vice-president from out of their midst. The
committee undertakes to find work for unemployed
members whenever possible, and this is the oftener
done owing to the association of the fund with the
municipality.

Though the Out-of-Work Insurance Fund of Berne
has been in existence so short a time, and relies
entirely for success upon the good sense and provident
habits of the working classes, it has unmistakably
established itself amongst the social institutions of
the town. Its promoters are more than satisfied
with the results achieved. I quote from an official
statement :—

"The Insurance Fund has justified its existence,
and it may be said with satisfaction that thanks to
its formation and operations its members and their

families have been protected against the direst forms of want during the winter months. Though the members are not numerous, we have good reason to anticipate an increase, especially as the wishes of the working classes and of the administrative committee have been almost entirely met in the new regulations, so that the continuance of the insurance fund against worklessness may now be regarded as assured . . . . That the fund is a great boon to the insured themselves is a demonstrated fact, but it is equally true that as a consequence considerably less demands have to be made upon the poor-law and police authorities on account of the worklessness of a large number of our poorer fellow-citizens. The opportunity of insuring oneself against worklessness is indisputably a better and worthier encouragement to self-help than any amount of poor doles can be. Nevertheless, it can only be regarded as a makeshift, and as an incentive to State, parish, and private individuals equally to endeavour to the best of their power to restrict worklessness itself."

These words may be judged in the light of actual facts and figures.

During the first year of the fund's existence 404 members joined, of whom 50 were struck off the books owing to arrears of contributions, so that 354 remained at the end of the year. Two hundred and sixteen members claimed relief, but as 51 soon found employment only 165 really fell on the funds.

The aggregate amount paid was 6835 francs (£253), the lowest individual amount being 6d., the highest £4 4s., and the average £1 13s. 3d. During the following year the number of insured was 390, but on the other hand 57 lapsed, leaving only 333 at the year's end. Two hundred and twenty-six members claimed relief, and 219 received it. The aggregate amount paid was 9684 francs (£379), in sums varying from 6d. to £4 6s. 8d., while the average was £1 16s. 6d. At the beginning of 1896 the total number insured had risen to 605.

It should be added that the Insurance Bureau also maintains during the winter a comfortable shelter, to which the unemployed may resort from 8 a.m. till 5 p.m.

Compulsory Insurance at St. Gall.

The cantonal law of St. Gall is dated May 19, 1894—the Law Concerning Insurance against the Consequences of Worklessness (*Gesetz betreffend die Versicherung gegen die Folgen der Arbeitslosigkeit*). This law empowers political communes to introduce, by resolution of the citizens, either for themselves singly, or in combination with other communes, obligatory insurance for definite or unlimited periods. The municipality of St. Gall, which is also the capital of the canton, is the only town which so far has put the law into force, though, indeed, it was for the sake of St. Gall that the measure was really enacted. In speaking of St. Gall's experiment it will be convenient to speak in the past tense, for though the insurance fund still exists at the time of writing these pages, it is doomed to extinction at the end of June, 1897, under circumstances to be explained later.

By this law the obligation to insure rested on all male wage-earners resident in the commune whose average daily earnings did not exceed five francs (or 4s.), while in the case of the better-paid workers it was optional. Workpeople of all grades in receipt of less than two francs (1s. 7d.) daily and also apprentices were expressly exempted, and though women might by law be admitted to the benefits of the Act by decision of the Town Council concerned, they have not been included at St. Gall. Where persons otherwise liable to insurance were already members of voluntary agencies conferring the same benefits, they were likewise exempted. Besides the premiums payable by the insured, the benefit-fund received a capitation grant from the municipal exchequer of 1s. 7d. upon all names on the books, realising the first year, with a membership of 4220, some £350; while deficits were shared equally by the municipality and the canton. The insured were classified in three schedules, according to the average wages received, and in these the premiums ran as follows:—

1. Where the daily wages did not exceed 3 fr. (2s. 5d.), 15 cent. (1½d.) weekly.

2. Where the daily wages did not exceed 4 fr. (3s. 3d.), 20 cent. (2d.) weekly.

3. Where the daily wages did not exceed 5 fr. (4s.), 30 cent. (3d.) weekly ;

the last-named amount being the maximum premium chargeable.

It is to be feared that the St. Gall fund was established without sufficiently full study and investigation of the subject in its practical bearings. Certain it is that in many respects the calculations of the promoters were belied by experience. For example, it was estimated that the insured would fall in the proportions of 20 per cent. to the lowest schedule, 60 per cent. to the second, and 20 per cent. to the highest. It was found, however, that the proportions were in the first year 68·62, 27·93, and 3·45 per cent. respectively.

The premiums were paid by means of special insurance stamps, affixed in a book, which was presented for control once a month. Exemption from the payment of premiums was granted to recipients of benefit, to sick persons on the production of a medical certificate, and to victims of accidents, unless they were in receipt of compensation under the Employers' Liability Act. Relief was only paid during total worklessness, and the rates were for the three schedules 1s. 6d., 1s. 8d., and 1s. 11d. per day respectively, so long as the funds allowed, and less according to circumstances, while the maximum period for which benefit could be claimed in any one year was 60 days. The money had to be fetched from the office at the end of the week, though persons on the funds were required to show themselves once a day for the purpose of control. Relief was, however, withheld where the authorities had reason to suppose fraud, when the "out-of-works" were rendered incapable of working owing to sickness or accident, when they were idle owing to their own gross fault, or owing to a strike, and also when, though able-bodied, they refused suitable work offered to them. The funds were also protected by the provision that to become entitled to relief the insured should first have paid premiums for six months uninterruptedly if natives, and for twelve months if foreigners.

The fund was managed by a committee of nine members, two chosen by the Municipal Council, and seven representing and mostly elected by the insured, though only Swiss citizens in full possession of their civil rights were eligible for election.

The aggregate amount of relief paid during the first half-year (January to June, 1896) that it could be claimed was £940, which was distributed in 2345 sums to 363 persons out of the 430 who had reported themselves as out of work. To January and February fell over half the relief, while June was almost free. As to the condition of the unemployed, over half were outdoor labourers, and three-fourths were married men. The duration of relief ranged from 5 to 60 days, and half of the recipients received it for 40 days. The highest amount granted was 126 francs (£5 0s. 10d.), the lowest was 9 francs (7s. 2½d.), and the average was 54 francs (£2 3s. 2½d.).

It is to be regretted that this experiment in compulsory insurance has had so short a trial. When it was adopted by the people of St. Gall it was with the proviso that if, a year and a half after its introduction, it should not be again endorsed by popular vote, it should expire in June of the present year. The institution was accordingly submitted to the *Referendum* last autumn, when the voting was adverse. The Municipal Council were, I understand, almost or altogether unanimous in the desire that the system should have a fairer and fuller trial, and so, on the whole, were the citizens generally, with the exception of those who were liable to insurance. The latter from the first kicked against the pricks of compulsion, because of the sacrifice which it involved. It did not take the better class of working-men long to discover that, admirable though insurance against worklessness was, a system which ranked them and unskilled labourers in common obligations was inequitable. It is probable that they would not have objected to insurance by classes —such classes being determined by liability to un-

N

employment, and each paying into and receiving from a separate fund—but to throw all workers together, without regard to the peculiar circumstances of their respective occupations, pressed hardly upon the higher classes of labour, which were in fact made to bear the burdens of others. This view of the question, supported as it was by practical experience, as the returns of the persons relieved showed, soon turned the artisans and better-paid factory workers against the experiment. On the other hand, the thriftless, hand-to-mouth-living labourers voted against it for the simple reason that they were on principle opposed to providence of any kind. Between them, then, these two classes of working-men—the "don't-need-its" and the "don't-want-its"—defeated the scheme on its re-submission to the citizens, and it must now be regarded as indefinitely suspended.

OBLIGATORY INSURANCE AT BASLE.

At the present time the Government of Canton Basle Urban is engaged upon the elaboration of a system of compulsory insurance of this character. I refer to the draft of a "Law Concerning the Establishment of an Institution for Insurance against Worklessness" (*Entwurf eines Gesetzes betreffend die Errichtung einer Anstalt zur Versicherung gegen Arbeitslosigkeit*). As a preliminary measure the

Minister of the Interior—following the judicious
plan of German Governments, of calling in the
advice of experts upon technical, and especially
economic questions,—requested Professor Georg
Adler, of Basle University, to prepare a report upon
the general question. This report, which is just
such an able statement as might be expected from
one who has made several notable contributions to
economic literature, was duly laid before a commission nominated by the Home Ministry, and
consisting of two Government officials (besides the
President of the Ministry, Government Councillor
Philippi), two professors, three employers, and three
workpeople. The result was a Bill laid by the
Minister of the Interior before the Council of State
last year, and since handed forward to, and very
favourably received by, the popular Chamber.

To the essential features of this Bill, whose speedy
enactment may, Professor Adler assures me, be
anticipated with tolerable certainty, inasmuch as the
Democratic (majority) party, the Conservatives, and
the Social-Democrats are all for it, I purpose drawing
attention. Rather than run the risk of failure by
overburdening this tentative law by a too pretentious
task, it has wisely been decided at present to restrict
insurance to two classes of workpeople. Yet these
two classes are at once numerous and pre-eminently
suited to become the object of an experiment of this
kind, inasmuch as they are peculiarly liable to the

conjuncture which the law is intended to meet. They are (1) factory operatives (as that term is interpreted by the Federal Factory Act of March 23, 1877), and (2) persons engaged in the building trades and in earth works of all kinds. In the first category are comprised employees in textile and knitting factories, chemical, machine, and tool works, breweries, tobacco and chicory works, and the printing trades and type foundries. In the second are comprised masons, stone-cutters, slaters, carpenters, joiners, painters, etc. With exceptions to be immediately noticed, the Bill requires all " dependent wage-earning persons who have lived for more than one year as citizens or settlers within the Canton Basle Urban " belonging to these two categories to be compulsorily insured against loss of work, on the completion of their fourteenth year, unless by the terms of their labour contract their occupation should be restricted to periods less than a week. The exceptions are (1) employees in receipt of wages of 2000 francs (£80) or more per annum; (2) apprentices and improvers under eighteen years of age in the manufacturing industries who are paid less than 200 francs (£8) per year; and (3) workpeople who can furnish proof that they already belong to an out-of-work insurance fund offering adequate help in the emergency contemplated. The first class are excluded on the assumption that they form the *élite* of the labour world, and are as a

rule, on account of their ability, in good demand,
and consequently but little exposed to any sudden
deprivation of livelihood. The second class are
excluded because they are believed to be for the
most part dependent upon parents and relatives, and
in many cases do not receive regular working wages.

It has been found in pursuance of careful statistical
inquiry—that 10,000 workpeople, in a population of
90,000, will at once come under this law in Canton
Basle Urban, that 18 per cent. of this number (or
1800—1000 in the building trades and 800 in
factories) is an ample and even excessive allowance
for the unemployed in one year, and that the
average period of idleness is 67 days. It is broadly
upon these data that the following scheme has been
elaborated.

Though only two classes of employees have been
chosen to experiment with, it has for evident reasons
been found unfair to treat them equally. In the
winter season especially, building and earth works
may for weeks together be at a complete standstill,
where the factories at worst may only have to run
short time occasionally.

This unequal liability to loss of work has been
met by a differential scale of contributions rather
than by any variation in the benefits offered. To
what extent will be seen later. In passing, it may
be remarked that the case of workmen who may
cease to belong to any of the trades which come

under the law has been foreseen; and it is proposed
to allow such to continue membership of the
insurance fund, and retain all the privileges connected therewith, so long as they fulfil the stipulated
obligations and do not leave the canton. Even
should such a workman change his domicile, he may
regain full membership on returning to his canton
and paying contributions to the fund for eight
successive weeks.

Two fundamental principles underlying this
scheme of insurance invite particular comment.
(1) As at St. Gall, insurance will be compulsory, and
(2) it will be restricted to such loss of employment
as is unavoidable, or, as the Bill has it, "guiltless"
(*unverschuldet*). It is held that a law of this kind,
to be of real use, must be obligatory in character.
Were it permissive it would offer no improvement
upon the voluntary system of indirect insurance
against loss of employment by means of trade and
benefit societies. Again, were the working classes
only partially insured, one of two undesirable
consequences might result. On the one hand, those
working-men who belong to occupations specially
liable to trade conjunctures might be apathetic
towards the law, in which case its usefulness would
be greatly restricted. On the other hand, were these
mainly to insure themselves, the premiums that
would be necessary to cover risk would be im-
practicably high, and the system would break down

from its own inherent unworkableness. There is,
however, another grave disadvantage in partial
insurance. It is not inconceivable that an employer,
finding himself under the necessity of discharging a
portion of his workpeople, would feel himself bound
in duty—as his employees would doubtless regard
him bound in justice—to dispense first with those
whom he knew to be secured against want by
membership of an insurance fund. Such a plan of
selection might be defended on broad humanitarian
principles, yet it would palpably entail hardship.
In Switzerland, moreover, there is the specific argument for compulsion that this principle—which is
an express recognition of the solidarity of the
interests of the labouring classes—underlies two
other industrial insurance laws now contemplated
by the Federal Government, namely, laws for
insurance against accident and against sickness.

It is also equally necessary that the only kind of
worklessness which should be contemplated by such
a law as this should be unavoidable and blameless so
far as the insured are concerned. Cases of sickness
and accident are excluded, since laws intended to
deal with them are now, as already stated, on their
way. The other disqualifications from receiving
relief laid down by the Bill are, (*a*) deprivation of
work owing to a wages dispute (with the exception
of a lock-out); (*b*) voluntary cessation of work;
(*c*) dismissal on account of wrongful conduct; (*d*)

refusal by the insured to accept other work when offered without adequate reasons, and (e) failure to pay contributions for twenty-six weeks without seeking to come upon the funds.

As to (a) it is contended that the refusal of relief when idleness is caused by strikes is imperative, since the State is bound to preserve an attitude of strict neutrality between employer and employed, between capital and labour. But this legitimate position involves as a corollary—and the Bill recognises it—that in seeking occupation for the unemployed the organ of insurance shall not accept work which is available owing to industrial friction. As to (c) the Bill, in order to protect workpeople against arbitrary treatment by unscrupulous employers, provides that the director of the insurance fund shall satisfy himself before refusing relief in such cases that dismissal was justifiable. Note as to (d) that it is not intended that an unemployed workman shall be obliged to take any work that offers. Regard will be had both to his proper occupation and to his social standing. A mechanic, for example, would not be refused relief because he was unwilling to do unskilled labour. At the same time power must be given to prevent sluggards from living at the expense of the relief fund.

Very few words as to the machinery of insurance are called for. In the interest of economy—and perhaps also of efficiency—the administration of the law is made as simple as possible. The executive functions will be discharged by a Director (*Verwalter*). This official will have a tolerably free hand, though he will be subject to the control and oversight of a Committee or Board (*Commission für Versicherung gegen Arbeitslosigkeit*) consisting of nine members,—three chosen by the employers, five by the workpeople, and the President by the Council of State. The Director of the Insurance Fund will be appointed for six years at a time by the Council of State on the nomination of the Board, and he will receive a salary ranging from 3500 francs (£140) to 5000 francs (£200). He will, of course, have a staff of subordinates according to requirements.

The Insurance Board will be nominated by the Council of State every three years, and its duties will be so far honorary that an acknowledgment of two francs per sitting is alone promised to members, and then only when they meet during work hours. This payment is explicitly made, indeed, not for services rendered, but as "indemnification for lost wages," and out of regard for the *amour-propre* of the Labour members the acceptance of the fee is made obligatory. With this Board rests, besides a general duty of control, the duty of decision in cases of dispute and of legal uncertainty, but appeal is allowed to the Council of State. Above the Board stands the Home Ministry, which is charged with the duty of keeping the Board and its ordinances scrupulously within the law. Both the employers and the workpeople sitting on the Board will be elected by their peers, but it is noteworthy that, democratic though the government and spirit of Switzerland in general are, female workpeople are not allowed to vote.

In fixing the amount of relief to be granted the originator of the Bill—for it should be stated in justice to Professor Adler that the Government virtually adopted his proposals as they left him —kept in view the consideration that idleness should not be made a desirable thing in the eyes of the unindustrious. Thus, to encourage the unemployed to search for work and to get off the relief books as soon as possible, it was found prudent, in dealing with the lower categories of labour, to guarantee a minimum subsistence only. On the other hand, it was recognised that among the unemployed there might and occasionally would be found superior workmen, with families, accustomed to a fairly advanced standard of life. To offer to such the relief which would be adequate for unskilled and unmarried labourers would be to mock their misfortune and to degrade them in the social scale. In each group, therefore, there are grades of relief, proportionate to earnings and thus to premiums paid, and also to domestic conditions—whether married or single, whether childless or otherwise. In the first place applicants for relief are to be

allotted to classes, according as the wages they have
received during the twenty-six weeks last preceding
the cessation of employment have been (1) 15 francs
and under weekly; (2) 15 to 24 francs, and (3) over
24 francs. Should a man during this period have
received wages falling to more than one of these
classes, the relief will be fixed on the basis of the
class to which his earnings mostly fall. The benefits
payable per day, counting Sundays and holidays, are
as follows, payment being weekly—

		First Class.	Second Class.	Third Class.
(a)	If unmarried	80c.	90c.	1f.
	If widower or widow without children under 14	80c.	90c.	1f.
	If married woman	80c.	90c.	1f.
(b)	Widower or widow with one or more child under 14, or married man without children, or with a child under 14	1f. 20c.	1f. 40c.	1f. 50c.
	Married man whose wife is in full work, or herself receives relief.	80c.	90c.	1f.
(c)	Married man with more than one child under 14	1f. 50c.	1f. 70c.	2f.
	The same if his wife be in full work, or herself receive relief	1f. 20c.	1f. 40c.	1f. 50c.

It will thus be seen that the relief offered ranges
from a minimum of 5·60 francs or about 4s. 6d. to
a minimum of 14 francs or 11s. 2d. per week.

With a view to saving the funds as much as
possible, and of encouraging workpeople to provide
independently against small emergencies, it is stipulated that no relief shall be payable for the first
week of worklessness. The general rule is also laid
down that relief may not be claimed for more than
thirteen weeks or ninety-one days during any one
working year (May 1 to April 30). To guard, however, against possible imposition, the reservation is
added that a member who has received relief for
fifty days or more successively in a working year can
only claim relief in the following year after he has
been at work, and has contributed premiums, for
twenty-six weeks dating from the receipt of the last
relief, though where a period of relief runs from one
year into another permission may be given to count
the whole to the earlier year. The case of workpeople whose wages are reduced owing to temporary
slackness of trade is fairly met. Where wages fall
more than one-half, two-thirds of the full relief of
worklessness will be paid, but where the reduction
is not so great no claim to help will be recognised.
An endeavour is also made to prevent unnecessary
calls upon the funds by a regulation providing that
where unemployed persons are able to earn small

sums by casual labour, relief may be reduced proportionately.

Following the example of most of the English trade unions the law further proposes to pay travelling money to cover railway fares up to 200 kilometres (and food by the way) to insured workpeople who leave home in search of employment.

Coming now, and finally, to the means by which it is intended to keep the relief fund replenished. Four sources of revenue are contemplated by the Bill, of which one, however—gifts and legacies—is purely supposititious and may be passed over at once. The other three are—(1) contributions by the workpeople insuring; (2) contributions by their employers; and (3) a State subsidy.

(1) Workpeople will contribute to the insurance fund according to the wages they receive. For the determination of their obligations the insured are divided into three groups—(a) workpeople who are not employed in the building trades; (b) employees of the building trades who are least exposed to worklessness; (c) all other employees of the building trades, who are in the main engaged in outdoor work. Each of these groups is again divided into three "wages classes" (*Lohnklassen*). How the members of the "wages classes" will contribute may best be shown by the following table :—

FIRST GROUP OF INSURED.—SMALLER RISK.

(a)	Weekly wages not exceeding	15f.	contribution	10c.	weekly.
(b)	Weekly wages of	15—24f.	„	15c.	„
(c)	Weekly wages exceeding	24f.	„	20c.	„

SECOND GROUP OF INSURED.—HIGHER RISK.

(a) 20c. weekly   (b) 30c.   (c) 50c.

THIRD GROUP OF INSURED.—HIGHEST RISK.

(a) 30c. weekly   (b) 45c.   (c) 60c.

These contributions will be deducted from their wages by the employers, who are required to pay them to the fund, along with their own contributions, every four weeks. Should a workman not have more than three days' work during any week he will be relieved of his premium, but should he work longer than three days, he must pay for the whole week. In the event of a workman being altogether without employment and receiving help from the funds, he will be exempted from the payment of premiums unless he be in receipt of compensation under the Employers' Liability Act.

(2) The employers' contributions are fixed at 10 centimes weekly for every workman of the first group of occupations in his employment, and 20 centimes for every workman of the other or more risky groups, with exemption in respect of all employees temporarily out of work.

(3) As an act of good-will towards an institution which it is hoped will prove of considerable public utility, the State is asked to bear the entire cost of administration, so that the whole of the contributions paid by employers and employed will be applied in relieving distress, and also to pay a further subsidy of 25,000 francs (£1000) per annum, which is to go towards the formation and keeping up of a permanent reserve fund wherewith to meet unforeseen emergencies. The State expressly declines any direct responsibility for the financial security of the insurance fund or the discharge of its obligations, though in the eventuality of passing difficulty it undertakes to advance a loan on interest. Yearly surpluses are to be placed to the reserve fund, but when this has reached 200,000 francs (£8000) the premiums payable may be reduced, or the benefits offered may be increased, as the Council of State may determine. Should deficits regularly occur, the premiums will be proportionately raised.

Such, in outline, is the scope of this important measure. The purpose of these notes is not critical, though some features of the Bill strongly invite criticism. Perhaps the objection first suggested is that this scheme of insurance excludes both the highest and the lowest categories of labour—the best and the worst paid, the *élite* and the "residuum." The difficulty of attaching the casual labouring class, with its migratory habits and its small and

uncertain earnings, to an institution which from
its very character can only afford benefit in return
for payment made, is obvious, and has indeed proved
one of the obstacles in the way of success at St. Gall.
It is not so clear, however, why the more highly
paid workers should not at least be given the option
of joining the insurance fund if so disposed. Again,
the claim that employers shall contribute to the
fund may well be justified on the ground of a moral
responsibility towards those whose welfare is so
greatly in their hands, and whose labour forms so
substantial an element in their commercial and
material success. There is just a fear, however, that
when an employer has helped to insure his workpeople against hardship from curtailed employment,
or none at all, he may deem his obligations towards
them to have ended. Who, with any knowledge of
the industrial life of our own country, or any part
of it—with any knowledge of employers as they are
in life, the employers of flesh and blood and not of
the Socialist *brochure* or the Hyde Park harangue,
has not come across multitudes of "capitalists," both
small and great, who, in spite of the "bloated" reputation of their order, prefer to make heavy sacrifice,
by working at an hourly accumulating loss, rather
than close their doors to the toilers to whom work
means bread, home, life? Human nature, good and
bad, is pretty much the same everywhere, and this
type of employer is probably no rarer in Switzerland

than here. Yet it is conceivable that under the
proposed law there might in times of bad trade be
less scruple than hitherto about running short time,
dismissing superfluous labour, or even ceasing work
altogether. In his defence the employer would be
able to point to the call made upon his pocket in
insurance premiums, and to the fact that even were
work quite cut off and wages wholly stopped there
could be no real want. The evil, however, would
consist in the change of relationship between employer and employed. This would be robbed of
much of the human sympathy which still remains
to it; it would tend to become hardened into a
merely formal tie between task-giver and task-doer,
between money-payer and money-earner.

But to say all this is simply to point out the
obvious fact that this Bill is not perfect. Nor is it
meant to be. Neither its author nor the Government which has accepted it claims that it will
diminish worklessness: it simply aims at lessening
the hardship and suffering which result from worklessness. Yet if only palliative, the Bill is practical,
and it will achieve good to the measure of its capa-
bilities. Professor Adler believes, indeed, that the
action of the Basle Government " will in all probability be of importance not only for the canton
but for the social reform movement in general.
Should the example of Basle succeed (as to which
he entertains no doubt) it will certainly be imitated

o

in other civilised societies, so far as they are in a
position to take in hand serious social reforms at all,
and soon will become general." In these words one
may detect the natural confidence of parental pride.
Yet however Dr. Adler's prophecy may fare, a scheme
of social amelioration which is thought worth trial
in the little country which long ago earned the
right to be regarded as the laboratory of political
experiment for Europe, merits respectful and studious
attention elsewhere.

CHAPTER XV

INDUSTRIAL LIFE INSURANCE

ONLY within the last few years have such facilities for life insurance as are offered by several English companies been placed in the way of the working classes and persons of small means in Switzerland. This is now done by the Swiss Life Insurance and Annuity Association (*Schweizerische Lebensversicherungs- und Rentenanstalt*), which in 1894 established a separate department for " popular insurance " (*Volksversicherung*) on a semi-philanthropic basis. In general the office is a " mutual " one, but no profit whatever is taken from the industrial branch, whose policy-holders, at the same time, are made responsible for contingent losses.

The principal feature of this branch of insurance is the payment of premiums by means of postage stamps, an arrangement allowed by the Federal Government in consideration of the excellent end in view. The stamps are attached to insurance cards, which are sent in once every three months with the amounts for that period. The Postal Department

exchanges the stamps for money, less a deduction of
one per cent. by way of acknowledgment for material
and services rendered. On the other hand the Association undertakes to surrender this branch of its
business, with all funded moneys, policies, and books,
etc., to the Federal Government on the latter's
demand at any future time.

Insurance is of several kinds. A person desiring
to take a policy may either be medically examined
or not as he prefers; in the latter case the
Association makes inquiries on its own account.
Where a person has been examined the sum insured
is paid to his relatives or next of kin at once and
unconditionally in the event of death. Where there
has been no examination the Association only agrees
to pay a third of the sum insured should death ensue
during the first year of insurance, two-thirds should
death result in the second year, and only the whole
sum after the insured has paid premiums for three
years. The reservations are waived, however, when
death is the result of accident and of various infectious and other specified diseases. Insurance may
be "mixed" or "life-long." In the first case (the
endowment system) the sum insured is payable at
death or on the attainment of a fixed age. In the
second case, though the sum is only payable at death,
the number of premiums is limited. The highest
sum insured is as a rule 2000 francs (£80). There
are periodical divisions of profits, in which all policy-

holders share who have paid twelve full quarterly premiums, and the bonus may take the form of an addition to the sum insured or a reduction of premium. Should a policy-holder be unable to keep up his payments, or desire for any reason to discontinue them, he may sell his policy back to the Association or receive one fully paid up for a reduced amount, provided he have paid twelve quarterly premiums. Lapsed premiums can, however, be resumed at will (on evidence being furnished of good health) during the next following twelve months on payment of the premiums due and a fine of three per cent. of the insured sum. Neither suicide nor death by duelling invalidates a policy.

The success attained by the institution so far has satisfied its authors, though the working classes have not been attracted to anything like the extent that might be imagined by any one familiar with the vast operations of the English industrial insurance societies. At the end of 1895 over 6000 policies had been taken out and 5108 (3524 males and 1584 females) remained in force, representing an insured sum of 4,495,265 francs, or nearly £18,000, an average of £3 10s. 5d., yet the lapses for 1895 formed the high proportion of twelve per cent. of the year's increase.

IV

POOR-LAW AGENCIES

CHAPTER XVI

HOMES FOR THE AGED POOR AT BERNE

THE *Greisenasyl*, or Old People's Refuge, is one of
the most beneficent of the philanthropic institutions
with which Berne is richly endowed. Originally a
private foundation, offering to a few aged people of
respectable antecedents a quiet home for the evening
of their life, it has come to be regarded more and
more as a sort of municipal almshouse, and on an
enlarged basis it is now wisely and successfully
managed by the authorities of the town. There are
probably few happier spots in Berne than the building in which nearly a hundred old men and women,
all over sixty years (which is the minimum age
of admission), most over seventy, and many well
over eighty, are housed, fed, and clothed without
care or anxiety on their own part. None of the
institutions which I inspected in that city in the
course of two special visits impressed me so favourably as this. It seemed to be the very realisation
of the ideal which is so largely an object of desire
and endeavour in England at the present time.

Whatever may have been the struggle of life which these pensioners have had to fight in the years that are behind them, they have now reached a haven of rest, and what is more, they know it and show it. There was not a sad face in the entire building. The brilliant sunshine which on the morning of my visit filled rooms and corridors, and made them look wondrously gay and cheerful, seemed to typify the moral atmosphere of the place. These veterans in years might have been boys and girls in spirits, so happy and contented did they look as they went about their light employments or whiled the time away in blissful idleness in the manner of those to whom hours and days have no longer any meaning. "Wie geht's, Frau ——?" ("How are you?"), asked my guide, Herr Bürki, the Poor Law Secretary, of one ancient dame in passing. "Herzlich gut!" ("Heartily well!") was the answer. And the radiant though toilworn and wrinkled face told that she spoke no more than the truth. Let me remark here that it was deeply interesting to notice the gladness with which Herr Bürki was received. Wherever he appeared he found himself immediately waylaid, stormed, and captured by grateful inmates. Old women would put down their sewing and knitting, old men would forget their pipes and newspapers, and even decrepit octogenarians would hobble forward from their chairs and quiet corners, all anxious to shake his hand and exchange a friendly

word, while such as were unable from infirmity to
leave their bedrooms bestowed their greetings
vicariously. This spontaneous evidence of the
esteem and attachment entertained by the municipal
poor for the representative of the municipal poor-
law spoke volumes for the humane and sympathetic
manner in which that law is administered in the
city of Berne. And when one thinks of it, why
should it be otherwise?

Work is quite voluntary in the Old People's
Refuge. But though no one is compelled to do
anything at all, every one is glad enough to have
employment of some kind. The men do gardening
in summer, wood-cutting in all seasons, with a little
carpentry in the workshop, while the women knit,
sew, mend, screen coffee, and take part in certain
domestic and culinary duties; but all on the understanding that they can begin, continue, and end just
when they please. For those who do not wish to
work there are books, magazines, newspapers, and
games, with tobacco for the men, and for the women
those tea-pots for two which stimulate gossip in the
known way. As for the meals, they are breakfast
at seven, a sip of wine at nine, dinner at twelve,
coffee at four, and supper (soup) at six. Where, as
happens in some cases, the friends of inmates are
able to contribute towards their maintenance, better treatment both in lodging and food is given.
Naturally the endowment of the Refuge lessens the

cost of its pensioners to the municipality. While the net annual cost of maintenance and administration for the whole of the inmates is 344 francs, or £13 7s. per head (rather over 9d. per head per day), the authorities of Berne pay only 120 francs (£4 16s.) each, though other parishes which send pensioners to the home, and a number do, pay from 150 francs (£6) to 200 francs (£8).

Another institution which, like the *Greisenasyl*, offers a home to many old deserving people, is the *Burgspital*, or Burghers' Almshouse, an ancient and wealthy foundation intended for the particular benefit, and under the control, of the freemen of Berne. The *Burgspital* possesses revenue-yielding property to the value of nearly £160,000, and altogether expends some £5400 a year on the Almshouse, and £600 in benefactions outside.

Several classes of inmates are received into the large and well-appointed building on the Christoffelplatz, above whose portal are inscribed the words " Christo in Pauperibus." There are (1) the ordinary beneficiaries (*Pfründer*), poor persons of both sexes, being free citizens of Berne, who are either wholly or partially incapacitated from earning their livelihood owing to age or sickness. To such, complete maintenance is afforded for the remainder of their lives so long as they stay in the institution and conform to its regulations. They can leave at will, but then they forfeit claim to further help. No payment is required, though the authorities reserve the right to recover recompense in the event of such inmates acquiring means or leaving estate. In so far as their strength allows, they may be required to do light work.

(2) There are then the extraordinary beneficiaries (*Extra-Pfründer*), from whom or from their friends a moderate yearly payment, together with one outfit of clothes, is required. They are subject to the same discipline and obligations as the former class.

(3) There is also a class of " Boarders " (*Kostgänger* and *Kostgängerinnen*). These are free citizens of Berne whose means are not sufficient to afford them an independent home, and who, owing to age or weakness, are incapable of remunerative employment, yet who, owing to their superior social position, merit better treatment than the ordinary pensioners of the Almshouse. These provide their own furniture and clothing, and also pay towards their maintenance, while in the event of such an inmate leaving means at death, the authorities have the right to demand an additional sum not exceeding half the sum already levied in maintenance. Naturally these boarders are allowed a wider freedom than the rest, and indeed as far as possible they are allowed to live in their own way.

(4) Sick persons—citizens of Berne—are also admitted with the exception of imbeciles and such

as suffer from venereal and infectious skin diseases.
As a rule the longest time allowed in such cases is
three months. In the sick-rooms are likewise received, besides the permanent inmates, domestic
servants and journeymen who have been living with
citizens of Berne for at least a week, military from
the barracks, and journeymen and women in transit.

The following figures for 1893 will give an idea
of the work done by the *Burgspital*:—

Class of Inmates.	Number.	Days of Maintenance.	Average.
Ordinary and extraordinary beneficiaries ...	58	19,681	339½
Boarders	44	15,204	245½
Sick persons (excluding permanent inmates)	394	12,145	31

The inmates are well cared for by the officials
and deaconesses who form the large staff of the
Almshouse. Their rooms are well furnished, there
are delightful gardens for promenade, a library is
open to all comers at all hours, while their bodily
ailments are attended to by a resident physician,
and their spiritual needs are met by a chapel and a
chaplain, one of whose duties, as laid down in the
constitution of the Almshouse, is to "aim at leading
the inmates to show a proper and grateful appreciation of the benevolent purposes of the institution."
Yet I am bound to say that I missed somehow the

tone of happiness and cheerfulness which prevails
so remarkably in the Old People's Refuge. Whether
or not the difference lies in the character of the
inmates, I am not able to determine. There may
be much in the circumstance that while most of the
pensioners of the Refuge are probably more comfortable now than ever they were, many at least of
the inmates of the *Burgspital* have seen happier
days. And as Dante and Tennyson sing, it is just
the remembrance of these that gives to sorrow its
keenest edge.

The same institution does good service, too, to the
city of Berne as a temporary refuge for such homeless people (*Obdachlose*) as are too decent to be packed
off to the Workhouse. Such remain from a few days
to a few months according to circumstances. As is
explained more fully later, the Almshouse also offers
nightly lodging to accredited journeymen and labouring men and women travelling in search of work,
and from its funds out-relief is paid to many needy
persons for whom room cannot be found in the
building.

CHAPTER XVII

THE CARE OF PAUPER CHILDREN

AMONGST the most welcome of the social signs of the times is the growing interest which is being taken in the question of the care and training of destitute and neglected children. The day when the Workhouse was thought good enough, and almost too good, for the little outcasts whose maintenance became by law a public responsibility has already gone by, and if yet our poor-law institutions do not fully reflect the altered public sentiment on the subject, the reason lies largely in legislative and financial causes, whose removal requires time and a considerable degree of adaptation. The cry of philanthropy nowadays is not "Take the homeless child to the Workhouse!" but, rather, "Take it anywhere else than there, for heaven's sake!" We are slowly learning to treat questions of poverty and poor maintenance on scientific principles—rudely scientific, it may be, yet scientific to the extent that it is recognised that certain psychological and physiological laws and forces enter into play, and that these need

to be understood and, as far as possible, allowed for.
We have, of all things, learned the truth that there
is such a thing as hereditary pauperism; that the
pauper spirit and inclination can be handed on from
parent to offspring, unless powerful counter-influences
are brought to bear against it. We have learned,
too, that nothing is more calculated to foster pauperism than pauper associations and surroundings. That
like begets like in the moral sphere is a fact of
appalling sureness and significance in Workhouse
experience. For generations this truth was un-
heeded, with the result that we made more paupers
than we relieved. Old and young were indiscriminately kept together in our poor-houses, and it happened inevitably that the young caught the pauper
taint so strongly that they were either unable or
unwilling in after years to detach themselves from
pauperising habits and tendencies.

Theoretically, at any rate, we admit that this
indiscriminate mode of treatment is radically wrong,
and here and there earnest attempts have been made
to improve upon it. In London, especially, the
Barrack system has been tried—a system under
which large numbers of children are brought up, fed,
housed, and educated under one roof. This, however, is a very wholesale and undiscriminating way of
dragging children up to a working age. It may be
economical, so far as mere cost goes, but apparent
financial success may in such a case be the worst

P

possible extravagance if ultimate results are considered. The Cottage Home system is another plan which has been followed here and there. It is an improvement upon the Barrack system; but here again there is the disadvantage that the children are stringently kept together instead of being allowed to associate with children and adults of the non-pauper class, with the result that their social prospect is never broadened. The system of Isolated Homes which the Sheffield Board of Guardians has adopted seems to offer even better promise of effectively counteracting the pauper bent, while the boarding-out system, given proper care and control, is probably the best system of all.

It is this system that Swiss towns have generally preferred, and their experience more than justifies the confidence which is felt in it. Lodged with foster-parents, there is nothing whatever to remind the children that to be the "children of the State" (or more truly the Rate) they must be children of adversity. Instead of being the automata of a relief institution they become members of a home, and generally a happier and brighter than any they knew under normal circumstances. Probably no towns of Switzerland have carried the boarding-out system to greater perfection than Zurich and Berne, whose arrangements are well worth studying. Not a single pauper child of either of these towns, nor yet of Basle or Geneva, of which mention will also be made in this chapter, is lodged in the Workhouse.

So implicitly do the poor-law authorities of Zurich trust the family idea, that where there seems a certainty that the children of destitute parents will be properly looked after by those parents, in the event of help being given, they allow them to remain in their natural custody, even though the cost to the town should be greater than with boarding-out. Where, however, the home influences and surroundings are morally unwholesome—where irregularity of living, roughness and slovenliness are to be feared —they are taken from their parents' or guardians' hands and placed with foster-parents in the country, and only when the children labour under serious physical or mental defect are they handed over to special institutions. In 1894, 293 children were maintained at the cost of the town, and of these 46 were in institutions of various kinds, and 247 were either foster-children or apprentices. The normal payment made to the foster-parents is 156 francs (£6 5s.) per year for children over two years, and 234 francs (£9 7s. 6d.) for children under two years, with, in addition, the cost of clothing, school appliances, and medical attendance when necessary. Only in exceptional cases is this rate exceeded: for example, when the child is sent not to the primary but to the secondary school, thus causing his guardian extra expenditure. As to this question of education, a, few words must be taken from the last poor-law report.

"In the relief of the poor at Zurich importance is attached to the sending of all supported children—in so far as lack of capacity does not make this impossible—to the secondary school, since thorough education is calculated greatly to facilitate their later progress. Where families are supported out of the public funds, it is required that the parents shall not be content with sending the children to the continuation school, so that they may be rendered capable of affording the family help with their small earnings, and may incur danger of various kinds by consorting with evil elements, as errand boys and the like, thus falling into sloth, and gradually becoming unruly and incapable of receiving a proper trade training. In regard to those who leave school, whenever they show suitability, care is taken to teach them a calling, and here the wishes of the children are considered as far as possible, with due regard to their capacities and to the resources of the poor funds. The necessary expenditure incurred in education and commercial training is certainly considerable. On the other hand, it cannot be sufficiently emphasised how important it is to help these children, by a thorough-going and efficient theoretical and practical training, to such a degree of independence that they will never need to claim public support in the future unless from their own fault."

Such enlightened words are in strange contrast to the niggardly policy pursued often enough by English Boards of Guardians, particularly in rural districts, in the matter of pauper education.

Directly the children are old enough they are apprenticed or otherwise put to service in town or country, and in 1894 no fewer than 74 (47 boys and 27 girls) were in training for practical life as bakers, hinds, designers, bookbinders, printers, engravers, gardeners, cooks, confectioners, painters, mechanics, butchers, locksmiths, saddlers, smiths, tailors, joiners, bootmakers, paperhangers, cabinetmakers, teachers, domestic servants, and nurses. In order to secure the due fulfilment of obligations, alike by foster-parents and employers, the children are periodically inspected by an official of the Poor Administration as well as by members of that body.

Zurich also possesses an admirable Municipal Orphanage (*Waisenhaus*). Subject to the decision of the Poor Administration it admits (1) children who have lost both parents; (2) children who have lost father or mother, if their relatives are not in a position to provide proper training; and (3), in exceptional cases only, children who, though not orphans, lack the necessary care and support. The minimum age of admission is four years, and the maximum age is 14 years, while the children are, as a rule, retained until the age of 16 years, when the boys are supposed to be ready for a trade, and the girls for service of some kind. The number of children admitted is limited at any one time to 100. The children receive a very careful training. The discipline is kindly and benevolent, though emphasis is laid on obedience and regular habits. Everything is done to foster the family idea. Life is made as varied as possible, and by picnics and days in the country in summer, and by reading evenings and musical and dramatic entertainments in winter, the recreative needs of the young are systematically ministered to. In regard to clothing and food, the idea is to bring up the children like children of the Swiss middle-class. Especial care is taken with their education. They begin at the primary school, but from this all likely children pass to secondary or continuation schools, and then again, in many cases at least, to special trade schools if thereby they can be aided in the callings which they are destined to follow. In the choice of these the evident capacities and tastes of the children are allowed free play. Where a child's responsible guardians are able to contribute to his support, the Poor Administration reserves the right to require a certain payment, though the amount is arbitrary. It is also stipulated that each child admitted to the Orphanage shall bring a sum of at least £2, which is deposited in a savings bank, and on the child's discharge it is used on his behalf. The Orphanage is under the control of a committee of the Town Council, but the practical administration falls upon a paid master and matron and a resident doctor, assisted by nurses and other attendants. At the beginning of 1894 79 children were in training, while 30 others were supported as apprentices. Of the 79, 36 were attending primary schools, 26 secondary schools, one a continuation school, and two higher schools. The year's expenditure was nearly £3000.

The system adopted by the town of Basle does not materially differ from that of Zurich. In so far as the children who fall upon the poor fund have not to be sent to reformatories of various kinds—like the Richter-Linder Institution, which enjoys a high reputation—they are either boarded out or brought up in the Municipal Orphanage. In no event do they enter a Workhouse or come in contact with adult paupers. The sum paid to foster-parents is about £8 a year, besides allowances for clothes in many cases.

In Berne the care of pauper children is regarded as one of the most important departments of poor-law administration. Here, too, the boarding-out system is followed; and in a conversation upon the subject the Poor-law Secretary (Herr Bürki) was very emphatic in his statement that no other system could be regarded as satisfactory. Over 800 children are now either boarded out or (if old enough) lodged with masters as apprentices at the cost of the town. The municipality has never any lack of applicants

for children, though the sum paid yearly is not large.
The scale is as follows :—

Age.					Yearly payment.				
First year			...	...	180 francs, or	£7	4s.	3d.
1 to 2 years			...	...	156	,,	,,	6	4	10
2 ,, 3 ,,			...	...	120	,,	,,	4	16	0
3 ,, 4 ,,			...	...	114	,,	,,	4	11	3
4 ,, 5 ,,			...	...	108	,,	,,	4	6	4
5 ,, 6 ,,			...	...	102	,,	,,	4	1	8
6 ,, 7 ,,			...	...	96	,,	,,	3	17	6
7 ,, 8 ,,			...	...	90	,,	,,	3	12	0
8 ,, 9 ,,			...	...	84	,,	,,	3	9	2
9 ,, 10 ,,			...	...	78	,,	,,	3	2	6
10 ,, 16 ,,			...	...	72	,,	,,	2	17	6

The country is preferred, if possible, because rural
life offers a better guarantee of effective oversight,
and less inducements to irregular habits. Before a
child is either placed with foster-parents, or (as apprentice) with a master, an inspector makes a careful
inquiry into the suitability of the home or service
offered. The result of this plan has been to reduce
to a minimum the case of removals on account of
neglect on the part of guardians. It is also the duty
of the inspector to make periodical visits to the
foster-parents, in order to learn by inquiry and observation how the children fare. The local clergy
further exercise unofficial oversight, and act as refer-
ences, and in this way a tolerably efficient control is
maintained, though the homes are scattered all over
the canton of Berne. At the present time Berne even
places its imbecile children (if the cases are not very

bad) in private houses, though the plan is not regarded as a desirable one, and a movement is on foot
for providing a special cantonal establishment for
dealing with such unfortunates.

At Geneva the municipality does not concern
itself directly with poor-relief, organised effort being
exerted through an institution known as the *Hospice
Général*, whose funds come from private sources.
The "Commission" of the *Hospice Général* is composed of 17 members, elected for four years, and
it in turn elects yearly an executive board, consisting
of a president, vice-president, and two secretaries.

There are three modes of dealing with destitute
children. (1) For orphans of both sexes there are
two establishments (*Maisons des orphelins*), one for
each sex, in which the little ones receive a thorough
education until they are able to go out into the
world and earn their own livelihood. (2) Children
of three kinds are also placed in large numbers
with foster-parents in the country—orphans, deserted
children, and children whose parents are not able
to keep them. Here, again, the administration of
the *Hospice Général* makes itself responsible for
their maintenance until they are of working age.
(3) There is also in Geneva an institution for abandoned children (*l'enfance abandonnée*), which is
carried on distinct from the *Hospice*, and is subsidised by the State. The definition of "orphan" is
neither wider nor narrower than at Zurich. "Those

children can alone be admitted to assistance by virtue of being orphans who fall into the following categories and are destitute of the resources necessary for their maintenance and education:— (1) Children without father and mother; (2) children without father or mother, in the event of the surviving parent's proved inability to provide for their education; (3) children morally neglected by their parents, when such neglect is officially established." When the children are placed with foster-parents the latter may be paid either in money or in kind, though it is most generally the former.

In 1895 the *Hospice* had no fewer than 209 children boarded out in private homes in the country or otherwise, more than half being located in the canton of Geneva; and it was also maintaining 37 apprentices in four different cantons, apart from 25 boys who were in training at the agricultural colony at Serix.

The Orphanages, however, play a most important part in the poor relief system of Geneva. Of a total expenditure of £23,807 on the poor in 1895, £3775, or 16 per cent., went to the relief of orphans. Children are admitted to the Orphanages from the age of seven years, and they remain until the end of their apprenticeship, or about the age of 18. Up to the age of 14 years attendance at the primary schools of the city is required, though if children show exceptional brightness they may be sent to a secondary school. For here, as at Zurich, the education is liberal, and from the same motive. "The administration seeks" (so runs the statute) "by all possible means to inculcate in the hearts of the children committed to its care the sentiment of duty and the qualities which make the honest and industrious citizen. Religious instruction is given to all, Protestants or Catholics, and on Sunday all the children are required to take part in religious service."

The food is wholesome, abundant and varied, and the meals are taken in common as follows:—6.15, breakfast, consisting of coffee and bread; dinner at noon, of meat, vegetables, and bread daily, with wine for the apprentices; 7, supper of soup and bread. The clothing is also excellent, and there is nothing to distinguish either boy or girl from other children of the community, for the administration (in its own words) "carefully avoids everything which might have the character of a uniform."

When the time comes for sending the boys out into the world—about the age of 14—care is taken that no round pegs fall into square holes. A trade having been provisionally selected, the boy is allowed a month in which to try his hand at it, then he may ratify the choice, or, if dissatisfied, choose another trade. The term of apprenticeship is three or four years, according to the technical skill to be acquired. At its close the boy is examined, and, if proficient, he obtains a journeyman's diploma. As a rule, it is arranged that the master shall pay a small gratuity weekly, part being given to the boy as pocket-money, and the rest accumulating in the savings bank for the purchase of tools or other labour requisites when he completes his service. To this the institution adds a generous outfit. It should be stated, however, that when apprenticed in the city the boys continue to be fed and lodged at the Orphanage until they have served their indentures. Not only so, but they remain subject to the guardianship of the *Hospice* until they come of age.

In 1895 100 boys and 49 girls were in these admirable institutions. Of the former 44 were still attending elementary schools, and 36 were apprenticed to various trades and other occupations. Of the latter 32 were attending elementary schools, and 14 were in service. The Commissaires state that reports are continually received from employers of both boys and girls attesting the regular habits in which they have been trained while in the Orphanages.

Apart from these official agencies there are many private organisations in Geneva engaged in the care of the neglected young.

The movement in favour of the treatment of pauper children out of the Workhouse is spreading in Switzerland. Quite recently a step in the same direction was taken in the canton of St. Gall, whose record in this respect is far from enviable. The credit for what has been done is largely due to the late

Dr. Sonderegger. This gentleman found on inquiry a year or two ago that a shocking state of things prevailed. In 65 Workhouses of the canton there were 699 children and young people. There was continual and harmful intercourse between old and young; as a rule, there was no separation of the sexes, insomuch that in one place an unmentionable condition of things was found to exist; and by general consent the system adopted was rotten and scandalous. Not only, however, were children thrust into the midst of adults of evil antecedents and unwholesome habits, but amongst the young there was no attempt at classification, and the orphan of honest parentage and pure home was brought up in the companionship of waifs and strays of the worst reputation. Dr. Sonderegger, backed cordially by Dean Kambli, of St. Gall (to whom I am indebted for facts upon the subject), zealously agitated the question on public platforms, in the Press, and in the Legislature of the canton. He demanded the entire removal of children from the Workhouse (with the reservation that establishments of the best class only might continue to house such inmates for three years longer) in favour of the dual system of boarding-out and training in special institutions, for which latter purpose he asked that poor-law unions should, where necessary, be grouped. The Legislature has not yet consented to accept the Sonderegger-Kambli programme in its entirety. All that it has decided is that henceforth no more children may be admitted into the Workhouses, but those already there may be retained. Naturally the party of reform, which is a large and growing one, is dissatisfied with this inconsequent makeshift, and it is likely that before long, in St. Gall, too, the present system of pauper-child maintenance will be revolutionised after the example of the more progressive parts of the Confederation.

It may be that boarding-out and the provision of special homes may entail somewhat greater expense than wholesale Workhouse treatment; but on the other side of the account there are assets which cannot exactly be expressed in pounds, shillings, and pence, and higher moral character, the development of a more vigorous manhood and womanhood, and the promise of more useful citizenship are among them.

CHAPTER XVIII

IT is hardly an error to describe thus the unique institution known as the *Armenanstalt*, which is situated amongst the hills at Kühlewyl, several miles away from Berne, since "Poor-house" alone, and "Workhouse" still more, fails to give an accurate idea of the place and of the position which it fills in the social economy of Berne. The Poor-house (for brevity's sake) was built some seven years ago for the reception of several distinct classes of inmates (not at all for children, by the way); principally for (1) persons permanently unable to work and support themselves, and having no means of subsistence, and (2) persons either altogether or partially unable to maintain themselves whose lodgment in such an institution seemed "justifiable in the public interest."

This latter phrase is a significant one. What it implies will be best understood from a passage in a report addressed to the Municipal Council Committee which, under the guidance of the mayor of the day

Herr Müller (now Federal Minister) formulated the scheme.

"We regard it," they said, "as of the greatest importance that there be established for Berne a Poor-house in which all such adult poor may be lodged to whom this mode of maintenance is suited. They include not only a large number of the infirm and incapable, but particularly all the good-for-nothings and depraved people who become a burden on public charity, whose conduct is a cause of annoyance, and who cannot be improved except by systematic discipline, by work, wholesome food, and regular life."

To speak without garnishing words, one great object was to clear the streets of Berne of the lazy and immoral of both sexes—people who could not, in a democratic country, be arbitrarily packed off to a prison, yet who were rightly regarded as social pests. The first of these two classes certainly far outweighs the second, but the second is by no means a small one.

Thus the Poor-house has much in common with the cantonal Workhouses, for whose establishment by the State a law of the year 1883 provides. According to this law, "The State shall establish Workhouses according to requirements; they are destined for the reception of (1) adult and able-bodied persons, who are yet lazy or of irregular life ; (2) persons under age, of bad character, and especially such as have been convicted."

The general character of the inmates may be judged from a classification of those newly admitted during 1894. Of these 64, 11 were sent to the house as convalescents (these being persons in receipt of poor relief), 29 were sent on account of age, sickness, or infirmity, necessitating chargeableness to the city, 10 by reason of confirmed inebriety and ill-behaviour, 9 by reason of homelessness, 4 on account of slight mental aberration. Probably the whole of the 330 to 350 persons who are continually detained here would on analysis be found to fall into these main categories in about the same proportions.

The site of the Poor-house is one of the very best that could have been selected. It is situated in a sequestered spot at the head of a valley, whose position affords just the isolation and means of effective oversight which are desirable in such a case. The locality is very healthy, the land is fertile, and there is an excellent supply of pure water close at hand. The whole estate consists of some sixty hectares, made up of cornland, meadow and pasture land, plantation, and a large piece of land set apart as kitchen and nursery gardens. The cultivable land is allotted to the growing of wheat, rye, oats, spelt, potatoes, peas and beans, cabbages, and onions, but a large portion is reserved for meadow and pasturage. The building, which was intended to accommodate about 400 inmates—some fifty more than the usual complement—is a plain but substantial erection, and the

Q

arrangement of the various departments has been admirably thought out. In no way is there association between men and the women, who both live and work in separate suites of rooms.

Unlike the Old People's Refuge of the same town, the Poor-house imposes upon all its inmates, both male and female, work suited to their strength and capacity, and it is in reality as busy a hive of industry as exists anywhere. Whenever possible a man is set to the trade which he has been accustomed to follow. For farm labourers and gardeners, for example, there is always a place. Where inmates have had no particular training the occupation in which they are likeliest to be most productive is allotted to them. Thus I noticed at work smiths, wheelwrights, cabinet-makers, strawplaiters, tailors, shoemakers, sempstresses, chairmakers, wicker-workers, bakers, paper-bag-makers, etc. It will be understood that a large part of the work done is intended for the house account. As a fact everything that is needed on the premises and the farm in the nature of food, furniture, wood-work in general, tools, sewing, and knitting, with repairs of all kinds, is done on the spot, and at the time of my visit looms were on order for plain cloth-weaving. At the same time a considerable sum is realised by the sale of articles produced by the inmates and by the farming of their labour.

The goods sold include chairs, wicker-work of various kinds, articles of straw, and paper-bags.

The farm is, however, still more productive. The stall of fat and flourishing cows—each with its own name, after the Swiss fashion—yields from 350 to 400 litres of milk daily, of which over half is consumed or used for butter, while the rest goes to the *Genossenschaft* (Co-operative Dairy) of the neighbouring village of Zimmerwald, there to be turned into marketable cheese at the rate of 11—12 litres of milk to one kilog. (about 2¼ lbs.) of cheese. There is, further, a large stall of Yorkshire pigs, which increase after their kind, and the sale of calves is also an important item. Without going into further details, the institution last year contributed by its industrial and agricultural branches, no less than 11,677 francs, or 33⅓ francs (£1 6s. 8d.) per head of the inmates, towards a maintenance bill of 55,296 francs, or 158 francs (£6 6s. 5d.) per head. Administrative expenses and interest on capital are here not reckoned.

The diet of the inmates, while betraying no leaning towards luxury, is ample and wholesome, and sufficiently regardful of individual peculiarities of health and constitution. Each person receives five times a day in winter, and four times in summer, a piece of home-made bread weighing 100 to 130 grammes, also nearly half-a-litre of milk; fresh meat or bacon is given twice a week (in amount 200 grammes free of bone), and vegetables (cabbage, potatoes, beans, pease, etc.), soup, and porridge belong also to the regular dietary. The mental and recreative faculties of the inmates also are not neglected, since, thanks to the kindness of private persons, books, magazines, and newspapers are provided in considerable number. Religion, as with Gretchen's Heinrich, would hardly appear to be a strong feature of the economy of this heterogeneous household. Church service is only held once a month, though in addition a local clergyman pays both men and women a fortnightly visit.

The appearance of the inmates, without exception, was that of health and content, and after passing through the establishment I felt able to endorse the words of the director, Herr Pulver: — "The people come here as a rule miserable and unhealthy, low and wretched, worn out by careless living and bad sustenance, but they soon become new creatures." One woman did, indeed, take me aside and pour into my ear a long tale of woe. But I was assured that the inmate was a victim of civilisation, who suffered from chronic discontent, and complained of exactly 365 different maladies in the course of every year. Another woman as we passed by furtively passed into the hand of my companion, Herr Bürki, the Secretary of the Berne Poor-Law Department, a petition whose pencil-scrawls had evidently been written with great pains. I must take the liberty of translating it—

" HONOURED SIR,—I must once more urgently
beg for my liberty. This institution is all well and
good for those who can find no home, and for unfor-
tunate mortals generally. Herr Pulver is good, and
the young woman S—— (an attendant) is very sen-
sible. But Herr Pulver will not give me any freedom,
and that is very sad for *young people*."

As this young person (who was well on the shady
side of forty) had caused the municipality expense
before her detention, which took place by virtue of
the exceptional powers already referred to, it is
hardly likely that her yearnings after freedom will
be gratified yet awhile. Nevertheless, her voluntary
praise of the institution which keeps her under easy
and salutary restraint is significant.

It was allowed by the municipal authorities that
much of the success, as well as thorough-going order
and discipline, of the Kühlewyl Poor-house is due to
the oversight of its efficient director, who is ably
supported by his hard-working wife, the matron. It
is Herr Pulver's plan to pick out the best men and
women in every department of work (except the
farm, for which several paid hinds have been engaged) and set them over the rest, and this devolution
of control and responsibility has acted remarkably
well. The result is that though he has every day of
the year to deal with a family of nearly 350 persons,
drawn in large part from the lowest classes of society,
such a thing as violent insubordination is unknown.

Certainly I was impressed by the remarkable order
which seemed to prevail throughout the whole establishment, and the smoothness with which, even in
the absence of the taskmaster's eye, industrial and
domestic operations alike seemed everywhere to pro-
ceed. Now and then, of course, a discontented spirit
gives rein to the natural man within him, but serious
occurrences of the kind are very rare. Should the
need exist, however, the municipal authorities possess
ample disciplinary powers, without having recourse
to the police, inasmuch as they can award cell detention up to ten days for inveterate idleness, drunken-
ness and other misdemeanours. The cells, which are
on the premises, are not, I must say, very formidable
places. It is noteworthy that no special uniform is
used in the Poor-house. The inmates are attired in
ordinary dress, without any attempt at symmetry,
though deserters, when returned, are stamped on the
coat as a warning. Several hours' leave of absence
is given once a week (on Sundays) to such inmates
as can be trusted not to abuse the privilege. There
is no control over their movements. The plan of
taking the inmates out in bands under supervision
was once, indeed, tried, but it failed. Now they go
alone, but each knows that in the event of miscon-
duct the liberty will at once be forfeited, and on
the whole their demeanour leaves little room for
complaint.

To refer briefly to the expense at which this

excellent institution is carried on. The Kühlewyl estate, as it stood at the time of the purchase, seven years ago, cost 115,000 francs (£4600). Additional purchases of land cost 70,300 francs (£2812), the building of the Poor-house entailed an expenditure of no less than 400,000 francs (£16,000), while 30,686 francs (£1225) went in the provision of farm buildings—a total for the real estate of 615,986 francs (£24,639). To this must be added 117,000 francs (£4680) for farm stock, implements, and supplies, tools, domestic utensils, and food and clothing stocks, so that the whole property represents now a capital value of some 733,000 francs or £29,320, on which interest of 23,550 francs or £942 is paid yearly. The entire expenditure for 350 inmates was for a recent year as follows—

	Total Francs.	Per Head Francs.
Maintenance	55,295·88	157·99
Administration	6,218·57	17·77
Interest on capital ...	23,550·0	67·28
	85,055·45	243·04
Deduct inmates' earnings of	11,677·19	33·36
Net cost	73,388·26	209·68
	(About £2935)	£8 7s.

The whole of this expenditure did not, however, fall upon the municipality of Berne. The Cantonal Government pays a subsidy of between £300 and £400 yearly on account of the large number of poor who flock to Berne from various parts of the canton, and there fall upon the rates. Further, a number of the inmates of the Poor-house have been sent thither by other parishes, which pay from £10 to £12 per head yearly for their maintenance.

From the hygienic standpoint the establishment must be regarded as singularly fortunate, thanks to an exceptionally favourable situation and to a careful *régime*. So healthy is it at Kühlewyl that convalescents in care of the poor-law department are often sent there for a few weeks, and the life generally sets them on their feet. The death-rate varies from 7 to 8 per cent., but it must be remembered that the inmates are as a rule middle-aged or elderly, and that a large part of them when admitted are physical and moral wrecks. Taking one year, 1894, the rate was 7·5, but of the 31 deaths 27 were of persons over 50 years, 20 of persons over 60, and 9 of persons over 70.

CHAPTER XIX

SHELTERS FOR THE HOMELESS

IN some Swiss towns of larger size—Berne and Basle among them—special provision is made for the temporary housing of homeless persons to whom the Poor-house, the Workhouse, or police-quarters are not suited. In Berne, for example, it is virtually impossible for either individuals or families to be thrown helplessly upon the streets owing to passing poverty or sudden deprivation of home. The needs of such are met by two *Nothfallstuben,* or Emergency-Rooms, and by arrangements which exist at the *Burgspital* or Burghers' Almshouse. The Emergency-Rooms are maintained by the town, which both finds the buildings and furnishes them, and also gives to an attendant in each place board and lodging (without salary) and a fixed fee per inmate (70 centimes to 1·20 francs per day) in return for services. The extent to which these simple yet useful institutions are used will appear from the following figures :—

233

Room I.	Women.	Days.	Children.	Days.	Cost. Fr.
1892.	34	644	129	2331	2552·00
1893.	29	516	74	1284	1731·30
1894.	14	228	98	1271	1448·80

Room II.	Men.	Women.	Children.	Days.	Cost. Fr.
1892.	23	1	5	272	255·50
1893.	11	1	5	246	246·70
1894.	4	—	—	36	107·40

The provision in the *Burgspital* is more elaborate,
and contemplates a longer sojourn than is usual in
the Emergency-Rooms, the duration varying from a
few days to a few months, according to circumstances.
In the eventuality of disaster by flood or fire, whole
families are housed and maintained for weeks
together in the rooms set apart for them in the
Burghers' Almshouse for this branch of its beneficent work.

CHAPTER XX

THE Children's Holiday Colonies (*Ferien-Kolonien —Colonies de vacances*) which play so large a part in the monotonous life of poor children in Germany during the summer months have for years been introduced in Switzerland, and at the present time they exist in connection with the primary schools of at least a dozen of the larger towns. A Holiday Colony does not entail great expense: it is, indeed, a singularly economical way of ministering both to the health and delight of children of necessitous parents. The usual plan is to select a suitable locality, generally at a considerable elevation—perhaps some such alps as the Sennen resort to with their herds of kine and flocks of goats during the short summer—and here the children reside in plain wooden erections or in tents in the absence of more substantial lodging. The life is of the simplest and most primitive: outdoor exercise all day long, weather permitting; rollicking fun from daydawn to sunset as only children understand how to make and enjoy it; with plenty

235

of rough pastoral fare, emphasis being laid on fresh milk. The children are taken in batches of from twenty to fifty, the sexes having as a rule separate colonies, and each child is sure of at least a fortnight's stay. Teachers accompany the troops of little holiday-makers, and share the common life and occupations of the colony.

A most laudable work is done by the philanthropic associations by whose resources and efforts the Holiday Colonies are generally maintained and worked, for municipal action seldom goes beyond the vote of a subscription to the requisite funds.

The town of St. Gall is, however, an exception. A special " Poor Scholars' Committee " of the Education Council conducts the whole arrangements for the relief of sick and needy children, collecting private subscriptions, despatching weakly boys and girls to their respective colonies near Rehtobel and Trogen (some 3000 feet high) for a residence of three weeks (not more than one being taken from a family), distributing soup as well as shoes and clothing whenever needed all the year round, and carrying on "milk stations" in the summer holidays. These last are five in number: at them needy children, who are not qualified for admission to the colonies, receive milk and bread twice a day (7 a.m. and 6 p.m.) for three weeks. In order to participate in any of these school benefactions parents must make formal application to the teachers on behalf of their children, and before decision each case is carefully investigated.

The town of Berne has had Summer Colonies since 1878, and some 300 children of the elementary schools are sent to them every year, the duration of the holiday being three weeks. The children are sent by recommendation of the teachers and public medical officers. The cost is barely £350 a season, or about £1 a head.

At Biel, in the same canton, forty or fifty children are similarly sent away, and here a large number of poor children are also supplied with milk in the town itself at various seasons of the year.

Two associations at Geneva set up five colonies every summer, and each of them receives from twenty to sixty children.

The Neuchâtel *Société des Colonies de Vacances* owns its own little estate at Bevaix, a village nine miles away, lying at an elevation of 1500 feet.

At Lucerne the institution of the Holiday Colony has also been placed on a permanent footing. There a small body of philanthropists have purchased a farm and built upon it a Holiday Home, which is used in July and August, when the tenant of the farm is bound by the terms of his tenure to dispose of all the agricultural produce that may be needed at the current market prices.

At Schaffhausen separate provision is made for poor children, and for those whose parents are able to pay; and here, too, special buildings are owned by the Society of Public Utility, under whose auspices the colonies are carried on.

It is, however, at Zurich that the system has obtained its greatest dimensions. The Central Committee of the Holiday Colonies not only sends children to nine stations in various parts of the canton, and of the cantons of Appenzell and St. Gall—all of them healthily situated at high elevations—but it has also carried on and owned since 1888 a permanent convalescent station at Schwäbrig, near Gais (Appenzell), which is open all the year round for the reception of both free and paying patients. This institution consists of a farmhouse and two dwelling-houses, having accommodation for a hundred children and thirty boarders. It acts, in fact, as a sanatorium for the debilitated youth of the town. Paying scholars are received on the strength of a certificate signed by a teacher and a doctor, and they are charged from two to three francs per day. Poor children are continuously drafted from the schools to the home, in batches of about twenty a month,—the normal duration of their stay,—and in order that the right ones may be chosen, the teachers are required to watch very carefully the health and nourishment of their young charges, and where impoverished circumstances are suspected to make inquiries at their homes. The ordinary Holiday Colonies are managed by five committees, one for each district of the town, with a central committee over all. At the nine stations some hundreds of children are received every summer for a period of three weeks, four teachers accompanying each contingent of from forty to fifty. Milk occupies the most prominent place in the children's dietary, and the time is divided between rambles and games.

Colonies are also provided in connection with the schools of Lausanne (two colonies), Vevy (three), Soleure (one), Aarau (one), Glarus (one), Chur (one), and elsewhere. One would think that some of these towns, both because of their delectable situation and their comparative smallness, were of themselves fit resorts for those in quest of health. That the philanthropic of their citizens think differently, when youth is concerned, must undeniably be attributed to a rare solicitude for the welfare of the young, and an altogether praiseworthy anxiety that even the poorest scholar shall at least be able to enter upon the battle of life equipped with a sound body as well as a sound education.   .

V

TECHNICAL EDUCATION

CHAPTER XXI

THE FEDERAL GOVERNMENT AND TECHNICAL EDUCATION

MANY years have passed since a leading public man in Switzerland said to one of the members of the first English Royal Commission on Technical Instruction : " We know that in this feeble country nearly the whole of the children will start out in life burdened with poverty, but we are determined that they shall not be burdened with ignorance also." It is not the purpose of these pages to consider the wise enterprise which the Governments and people of Switzerland have shown, and the generous sacrifices which they have made, in the cause of education generally, though both are infinitely to their credit, but rather to inquire into the technical side of the Swiss educational system, and its bearing upon the native industries and trades. It is generally worth a country's while to follow the commercial movements of its neighbours, and those of energetic little Switzerland, though she may not count amongst England's least negligible rivals, have latterly been very instructive. This, chiefly, is to be remarked, that the Federal Government has taken trade and industry under its protecting ægis almost more completely than any other Continental Government —not excepting that of Germany herself—whose diplomatists, with all their official decorum, are never above engaging in a little dignified commercial touting when chance or Providence puts them in the way, and whose consular service is both meant to promote the home trade, and, what is more, does it. For some years the Federal and Cantonal Governments, true to the conception of the State as the *mater benigna* which is becoming so popular in Switzerland, have left no stone unturned in the endeavour to prosper the commercial activities, and thus the material interests of the population. Nor have these new responsibilities been assumed unwillingly, as is proved by the growing readiness to vote public funds when outlay on this behalf is called for. No doubt the supposition is correct that the Governments recognise that in a healthy and progressive condition of commerce lies one of the greatest safeguards of social peace and contentment. The methods pursued are various, as, for example, the liberal subsidising of technical schools of all kinds, and even of technical journals, the formation of commercial museums and travelling sample collections, active solicitude for the home industries, which still afford employment for so large a part of the rural and semi-rural population, and the promotion of periodical exhibitions of native products of the industrial arts, etc., among which may be named those of Zurich (1890), Basle (1892), and Geneva (1896).

These measures are all an immediate outcome of the policy of State promotion of technical instruction which was initiated in 1884. Before that year technical, trade, and industrial institutions received no direct help from the Confederation, and the cantons were left to go their own way. Yet technical education was not a new thing in Switzerland, for it existed in a primitive and tentative way as early as the middle of last century. The towns which led the way were Geneva and Basle, which probably learned by French influence and example. Indeed, when the first *École de dessin* was founded in the former town in 1751, it was by the help of a Paris engraver. Supported heartily by the municipal authorities and the commercial classes, it speedily became an efficient and popular institution, and it may be regarded as the original of the existing *École municipale d'art.* Eleven years later (in 1762) Basle followed with a Public School for Drawing, which also has a lineal descendant in the *Allgemeine Gewerbeschule*—a cantonal institution of the present day. Berne came very closely after (1766); then Zurich (1773); and Winterthur and St. Gall were not far behind, and in all cases simple drawing schools

were the precursors of schools of wider and more
strictly technical range, as the teaching of art was
followed by practical training in its application to
industry. During the first half of this century the
less industrial parts of the country followed suit,
until, when the Federal Government stepped in,
there was scarcely a canton without schools and
other institutions for the promotion of certain
branches of technical instruction. The aggregate
number was, nevertheless, small, and the resources
with which they worked were inadequate. The
chief gain so far was that belief in technical education
had taken a powerful hold of the people.

A beginning in Federal enterprise was made when
the new constitution of September 12, 1848, gave to
the Confederation power to "establish a university
and a polytechnic school." The latter was undertaken
at once, Zurich being chosen as the seat, and it was
opened in 1855. Then the Federal Executive fell
again into the background, and the cantons and
municipalities were left to carry on the work of
technical education independently as before. Not a
few institutions and societies pursuing this end were
formed during the next two decades, and the movement continued to grow. On the conclusion of the
Commercial Treaty of February, 1882, between
Switzerland and France, however, the Federal Government instituted a far-reaching inquiry into the
condition and needs of native industries, both great

and small. The result was to bring to light the existence of a general and very strong desire for prompt legislative measures for the improvement and extension of agencies for technical instruction. This was speedily complied with, and the memorable "Federal Resolution (*Bundesbeschluss*) concerning commercial and industrial education," bearing date June 27, 1884, was drawn up as the basis of future federal action. The first article of this resolution set forth that "For the promotion of commercial and industrial education the Confederation undertakes to pay subsidies from the Federal Treasury to the institutions established for the purpose of imparting such education." The institutions especially recognised as belonging to this order were artisans' schools, commercial continuation and drawing schools (including those carried on in connection with elementary schools), higher industrial and technical institutes, art and special trade schools, collections of designs, modelling and teaching apparatus, and commercial and industrial museums. The Federal contributions were to go as far as half the sums paid on the same behalf by cantons, parishes, corporations, and private persons together, and in consideration of giving this help the Confederation, through the Department for Industry and Agriculture, was to exercise certain powers of control, both direct and by means of inspectors.

It was, however, stipulated that the aid given by the

Confederation should not diminish other efforts made hitherto, but should rather be regarded as auxiliary, and as a means of securing greater efficiency. One very important feature of the scheme was the formation of collections of models and the productions of the art-industries, with provision for their exhibition in various industrial centres.

Few of the technical institutions existing at the time of the Resolution coming into operation failed to place themselves under Federal protection and supervision by claiming the available grant; while an immediate result was to encourage the establishment of a multitude of new ones. No fewer than 92 sprang up in the first year, of which 61 were industrial continuation schools, artisans' schools, and drawing schools, the whole embracing 21 of the 23 cantons. Since then the Government has again and again multiplied its grants. From some £1700 in 1884 they have risen in 10 years to £20,601 (1894), and the total amount of Federal money thus employed during the decade exceeded £145,000, which in a country of Switzerland's limited resources is substantial indeed. As to the multiplication of institutions, while in the financial year 1884-5 the Government gave help to (1) 20 technical schools, (2) 61 industrial continuation and drawing schools and artisans' schools, and (3) 10 industrial museums and collections—a total of 91 institutions—the numbers in 1895 were 160, 38, and 13 respectively, a total of 211, though many of the higher schools and colleges in the latter totals have several distinct departments.

A remarkable result of the new life thus given to the system of technical instruction was seen in the National Exhibition of the works of pupils of subsidised continuation schools, artisans' schools, and industrial drawing schools, which was held in the Zurich Polytechnicum in September, 1890, under the direct auspices of the Federal Department for Industry. The entire cost of the exhibition, including carriage of exhibits by rail or post, was, in accordance with the democratic custom of the land, defrayed by the Confederation. Two years later the further progress made under the improved order of things enabled another class of technical institutions—the subsidised art-industrial and technical and industrial schools, and the training workshops—to give an exhibition of their capacity, and this was done under similar conditions at Basle in September, 1892. The still more pretentious exhibition which was held at Geneva in 1896 was really complementary to the two which preceded, for it was meant to afford to Swiss industry universally an opportunity of justifying itself both to the country and to the world.

At the present time the technical schools and institutions of all grades are a goodly array. It is the proud boast of Switzerland that none of her industries is without efficient agencies for providing the requisite special study and training, and better still, these agencies are, as a rule, situated exactly where they are wanted, having indeed been established to meet local needs. Watch-making has preparatory schools at Soleure, Biel, Neuchâtel, St. Immer, La Chaux-de-Fonds, Loëche, and Geneva; for weaving there are schools at Wattwil and Wipkingen (silk); for metal-working at Winterthur; for wood-carving at Brienz, Brienzwyler, and Hofstetten; for stone-cutters at Freiburg; and there are schools for dress-making, pottery, architecture, toy-making, smaller mechanical crafts, basket-making, and the railway service (Biel), with trade schools for women especially at Basle, St. Gall, Freiburg, Berne, La Chaux-de-Fonds, and Geneva—these being also intended for domestic training.

Some of these schools were established for the express purpose of preventing the decay of ancient house industries which had been unable to cope with the competition of power machinery. Here and there a certain amount of success was achieved in such cases, but even where the hope was not realised the schools adapted themselves to other ends, and on the altered lines have continued to the present time. Such a school is the weaving school of Wattwil, in Canton St. Gall, from a letter received from whose head-master I quote the following:

" The school was established (in 1881) in the hope of re-invigorating the house industry of hand-weaving, which numbered from 7000 to 8000 looms in the Togenburg (an industrial valley some twenty-eight kilomctres in length), which at the time had fallen into decay. This, however, was in vain; the competition of the machine-weaving works was too much for the house industry, which at some seasons of the year was unable to fulfil orders. Moreover, the more intelligent and energetic workpeople turned their attention to the more remunerative occupation of embroidering—likewise a house industry—which began at the same time. At the present day there are not more than from 200 to 300 hand-looms at work in the valley, but the machine-weaving works have been greatly assisted by our school by the training of capable men, both manufacturers and workpeople. The female population is mostly engaged in weaving, the male in embroidery. Now the manufacturers are able to derive special benefit from the school, since they can not only obtain advice as to the introduction of articles hitherto unknown to them, but they are able to obtain from the school workpeople who are fully equipped with new ideas."

As a set-off to this, the following incident may be mentioned. In 1894 the practical workers in the watch-making trade in the South opposed a proposal to establish a school of watch-making for women and girls, on the ground that it would increase competition and take work away from the present members of that somewhat hard-beset handicraft.

There are also training workshops for various handicrafts at Berne, Pruntrut, Geneva, Lucerne, La Chaux-de-Fonds, and Zurich; while the larger and more general institutions include the great Zurich Polytechnicum, and the Industrial and Art-Industrial Schools at Zurich, Biel, Winterthur, Burgdorf, Berne, Basle, St. Gall, Freiburg, Geneva, La Chaux-de-Fonds, and Lucerne. To this list of what may be regarded as higher institutions must be added the Industrial and Commercial Museums, admirably representative of local or cantonal industries and handicrafts, as well as containing general exhibits, at Zurich, Winterthur, Freiburg, St. Gall, Berne, Basle, Lausanne, and Geneva, and the collections of samples and models at Aarau and Chur. The primary technical schools—industrial "special schools" (*Fachschulen*), industrial continuation schools, (*gewerbliche Fortbildungsschulen*), artisans' schools (*Handwerkerschulen*), and industrial drawing schools (*gewerbliche Zeichnungsschulen*)—cover the whole country and are to be numbered by the hundred. In the towns the curriculum is as a rule more liberal than in the rural districts. Drawing (freehand, geometry, and perspective), arithmetic, history, mechanical and technical drawing, book-keeping, commercial geography, composition, modelling in plaster, stenography, chemistry as applied to industrial purposes, wood-carving, architecture, gardening, agriculture, modern languages (only

French and German), sewing and mending are taught, the average range being six or eight specific subjects. Most of the schools are carried on all the year round, and the remainder only during winter. In a large number no school fees are charged, and in some cantons attendance is compulsory up to a certain age.

Probably the larger towns of Switzerland are better provided with technical schools than any other towns of the same size in the world. Zurich, of course, stands pre-eminent with its Polytechnic, whose fame and work are too well known to need more than mention here. But though the greatest, this is not the only institution for promoting technical instruction at Zurich. There is also an Industrial School which in its turn acts as the centre of an important educational work. In connection with it are carried on industrial continuation schools in all the five wards of the city; a special artisans' school; a workshop school for wood-workers, and an art-industrial school, together with an industrial museum. These schools are all communal both in management and cost, and instruction is free, though a charge is made for books and other materials. In the industrial continuation schools the subjects taught comprise freehand drawing, geometrical drawing and perspective, mathematics, languages (French, German, and Italian), history (including constitutional history), composition, writing, with needlework for the female scholars. The schools are carried on all the year round and in the winter term give instruction to over 1000 young people and adults. The artisans' school is more practical in character, its curriculum comprising book-keeping, mechanics, chemistry, physics, gardening, and special theoretical instruction for joiners, cabinet-makers and upholsterers, wood-turners, masons, tinsmiths, locksmiths, mechanics, paper-hangers, gardeners, tailors, and shoemakers. Some 600 students attend each term. The workshop school for wood-workers does in practice for its pupils what the artisans' school does in theory. At this school young men may thoroughly equip themselves for the position of journeymen, for the term of training lasts from the age of sixteen to that of twenty. Zurich also possesses a silk-weaving school, which, however, is not free, fees of £6 for Swiss students and £12 for foreigners being charged for the first year, and £12 and £20 respectively for the second. There is also a school for laundry-work, in which fees are likewise paid. The art-industrial school aims at qualifying young people of both sexes for callings in which artistic training and taste are requisite. A small fee is charged, but those unable to pay are received free.

The technical institutions of Berne are hardly less numerous. Besides a workshop school for several handicrafts, there are an excellent artisans' school, an art-industrial school, and a school wherein women and girls are taught needlework of various kinds, knitting,

mending, and laundry work, as well as the usual
continuation schools, attendance at which is compulsory. The artisans' school is especially worthy of
mention. It has existed since 1829, and with its
comprehensive curriculum is admirably fitted to train
young men who intend to follow such handicrafts as
afford scope for originality and a cultivated taste.
The fees are quite nominal—5s. for the winter term
and 3s. 4d. for the summer. In the winter months
of 1895-6 nearly 700 students were in attendance.

Basle possesses an important Industrial School,
which has been the prototype of many similar
institutions in Switzerland. It dates from the end of
last century, and was long carried on under private
auspices, but now for a number of years it has been
managed by the municipality. The school is divided
into three departments. The primary department
is intended for young people who have just left the
common schools, and in it there is no specifically
technical instruction beyond drawing. The upper
department aims at qualifying persons of more
advanced years for following such local industries as
require artistic training, and the curriculum comprises
some sixty subjects. Here there are special courses of
theoretical instruction for cabinet-makers, locksmiths,
paper-hangers, book-binders, and others. The third
or female division is for art only. There is also at
Basle a useful "school for women's work," whose
scope is somewhat wider than that of the similar

school at Berne. Here pupils who have attained a certain degree of skill are given modest remuneration for the sewing done in school hours, for this is either done to order or is afterwards sold.

What is true of North Switzerland is also true of the South. At Geneva there is the same excellent system of technical instruction. The Professional Academy (*Académie professionelle*), the Municipal Schools of Art (*Écoles municipales d'art*), the Industrial Art School (*École des arts industriels*), the Watch-making School (*École d'horlogerie*), the Mechanics' School (*École de mécanique*), and the Evening Schools (*Cours facultatifs du soir*) are model institutions, all calculated, each in its way, to meet the local needs of industry and commerce. Except in the Industrial Art School, which is free, low fees are charged, though the junior students and those whose means are limited are offered gratuitous instruction.

It should be added that the Department for Industry—through whose hands the Federal subventions to technical education pass—is aided in its work by a Council of Experts, formed of acknowledged authorities upon education, art, industry, and trade, which is divided into groups dealing respectively with technical institutions pure and simple, art-industrial institutions, and industrial continuation schools. These experts on occasion visit foreign countries with a view to studying and learning from their work in the same sphere of education.

CHAPTER XXII

THE WORKSHOP-SCHOOLS OF BERNE AND ZURICH

No one can inquire into the system of technical education which has been set up in Switzerland without noticing how systematically the plan has been followed of adapting such education to local needs. Where certain industries have become characteristic of a locality, studied efforts have been made to render these more efficient rather than to offer indiscriminate facilities for improving technical knowledge without regard to its definite application. This has been the case in an especial manner with the house industries. Not a few of these have been preserved in a condition of vitality, and even of healthy vigour, by the timely provision of schools in which their hardly-pressed workers were able to acquire improved technical knowledge and skill, thus fortifying themselves for the keen competition of the modern machine industry. The same thing has also been done in various parts of the country for common handicrafts which were likewise threatened by machine production, and in this connection two agencies are deserving of particular mention and study. I refer to the workshop-schools of Berne and Zurich, which are, I believe, almost unique in their way. `

THE BERNE WORKSHOP-SCHOOLS.

The institutions (whose native description is *Lehr-werkstätte*—literally, "training or teaching workshops") to which I have given this name form a most important part of the admirable and extensive system of technical instruction which is carried on in the city of Berne under cantonal, municipal, and private auspices. My visit to the schools was paid in the summer of 1896, when I had the advantage of the company of the able and courteous director, Herr V. Haldimann, who was unremitting in his desire to make known all sides of his work. The schools date from the year 1888, and are now located in a large and handsome suite of buildings, formerly used as an asylum for the blind. They are a carefully-matured fondling of the Town Council, which has never from the first wavered in its belief, not only in their efficacy, but in their necessity, at least for Berne, and in that spirit has generously provided the somewhat ample financial means which they require from year to year.

The avowed purpose of the workshop-schools is

to place within reach of young people a thorough training, both theoretical and practical, in one of four common handicrafts. These are shoemaking, cabinet-making, locksmithry, and tinning. The apprentices are boys taken raw from school, and young men who have served their indentures in practical work and desire to go through the theoretical grounding which should have been acquired beforehand, yet which has from various causes been omitted. A collateral aim, however, is to increase the efficiency and vitality of the handicrafts concerned, by keeping their members abreast with modern methods and appliances, as well as with the requirements of modern taste, with a view to the advancement of native industry and the more effective combating of foreign competition.

The apprentices are of two classes—those who lodge on the premises, and those resident in the town, and, as a rule, there are about as many of one class as of the other. To both classes the municipality offers a free course of training in the handicraft chosen, with free insurance against accident, and (after the first six months) a moderate recompense for all work done beyond a prescribed normal output. This last is reckoned up at the end of each month, and from 50 to 75 per cent. of the amount found to be due is at once paid, the rest being allowed to accumulate until the apprentice completes his course. In this way it often happens that young men, on leaving for positions elsewhere, take away as much as £6 or £10, which to a young workman means a great help in the way of tools. Boarders pay for their food and rooms, but the sum charged is very small and does not, in fact, cover the cost, though, on the other hand, they do not receive premiums for work done. Shoemakers and cabinet-makers pay £10 a year for three years for board, and tinners £16 for the same period. The whole of the apprentices receive dinner free six days in the week, though more for the sake of order and economy of time than from any idea of benevolence. In order to secure as far as possible the right kind of pupils, the authorities as a rule prescribe a month's probation before the signing of indentures, at the end of which it is open to either side to complete the arrangement or not at will.

Beginners are set to light work; but both in theory and practice the students are led on regularly from stage to stage, with a view to affording them an intelligent all-round training. Each day has its due share of theoretical and practical work. The former naturally varies according to the handicraft followed, though some class subjects are common to all. The teachers are skilled men, for the work of the schools is carried on under the immediate gaze of the public, and periodical examinations test the quality of the instruction imparted. In the practical department the apprentices are divided out amongst working overseers, each charged with the training of a small number (from six to ten), so as to leave no room for wholesale treatment. There is no mistaking the excellence of the training and also of the results. The work done in the wood- and iron-work departments especially is of such a high quality that there is always a superfluity of remunerative commissions in hand. The shoemaking and tinning branches are naturally the most unpretentious. The former works especially for Berne— some 400 of whose citizens are regularly shod by the municipality; while the tinware produced is for the most part disposed of to a few wholesale dealers. Here let me say that there is no underselling. The goods produced are sold at a fair market price, which, owing to the uniform excellence attained, there is seldom any difficulty in obtaining.

The Workshop Order is systematic without being too stringent. Ready obedience is required of the apprentices towards their teachers and overseers, and it is as a rule given. The hours of work are 57 a week, of which from 44½ to 47 fall to practical work in the workshops, and from 3 to 9½ to instruction, including theory, drawing, model-cutting, arithmetic, and book-keeping. Every apprentice has to keep his own bench and tools in order, while the cleaning of the workshops and machines is done collectively. Neither smoking nor the drinking of spirituous liquors is allowed on the premises.

There is a separate House Order for the boarders.
The half-hundred apprentices rise at six, and half-
an-hour later they must present themselves neatly
dressed in the dining-room. Breakfast over at seven,
work begins at once, and continues until dinner,
which claims a pause from 12 to 1.30, the spare time
being passed in the open air as far as possible. Work
then continues until 7.30, when supper is laid.
Pupils of the Berne Artisans' School attend the same
at eight o'clock, and the others may read, play games,
or by permission visit the town until 9.15; 9.45 is
the bed hour, and at 10 the establishment is supposed to be quiet for the night. These times apply
to all the week-days alike. Sunday is, of course, a
free day.

The Workshops are managed by the Town Council,
which appoints yearly a special committee for the
purpose, under which the responsible director, his
overseers, and his teachers act. The working staff
at present includes, in addition to the director, a
book-keeper and a salesman. Shoemaking—a practical overseer and two teachers. Cabinet-making—a
practical overseer, three practical teachers, a master
turner, and a storesman. Locksmith's department
—a practical overseer, and three practical teachers.
Tin-working—an overseer, and two practical teachers.
The number of students at the end of 1896 was 90
(representing over 30 places), made up as follows :—
12 shoemakers, 28 cabinet-makers, 31 locksmiths, and

19 tinsmiths.   The expenditure on the whole establishment in the same year—not counting the building—was nearly £6000, including £1874 for salaries, and £1500 for raw material, but the sale of products realised £2300, and the deficit was made up by subsidies as follows :—The Confederation (part of the Federal grant on behalf of technical education) £893, the Government of the canton of Berne £933, and the Corporation of Berne £931.

That the Workshop Schools of Berne are doing a good work in promoting industrial skill is allowed even by their enemies, for these exist in certain of the private *entrepreneurs* of the city, who complain of competition and would be better pleased if the schools could be made to consume their own commodities instead of selling them.   It cannot be denied that this competition exists, but I have been assured that it is certainly not due to any paring down of prices on the part of the schools, but is rather a competition of high-class products with products which are seldom, if ever, better in quality, and often very inferior.   On the other hand, the industries cultivated are greatly benefited by the sending into the labour market of workmen thoroughly equipped with theoretical knowledge and practical skill, and, what is of at least equal importance, trained to be conscientious and to hold in a certain holy horror every appearance of scamp-work. The fact that the establishment has taken high diplomas at the Swiss National Exhibition of Arts and Industries tells its own tale.

I was informed that with the object of learning the precise degree and kind of help which the institution had afforded them, an invitation was recently extended to former pupils to send to the director of the schools an account of their experience since entering practical life. The reports which were received as a result testified not merely to the thoroughness of the instruction given, but to its sufficiency to enable students of normal capacity to fill situations in the widest spheres with success, and with satisfaction to their employers. This is the object with which the schools were established, and so long as it is achieved it will be continued, even in the face of interested opposition, which, after all, if given free play would be the death of most excellent institutions.

The Zurich Workshop-Schools.

The town of Zurich possesses a similar institution, though on a much smaller scale. I refer to the Workshop School for Wood-workers. It is hardly necessary to speak of it at length. Here likewise a thorough theoretical and practical training is afforded to youths desirous of following cabinet-making, particularly in its artistic branches. The school is a department of the Art Industrial School

of Zurich, and is under the director of the establishment, who has at his service several teachers and
master cabinet-makers. Apprentices are admitted
at the age of sixteen, and they must enter into
indentures binding them to remain for the full
course of four years. The school is carried on all the
year round, without interruption for holidays, as this
would interfere with the paid work which is done,
though, on the other hand, the apprentices have
a right to claim a fortnight's leave in the year.
The number of apprentices varies from 20 to 25.
Instruction, as at Berne, is practically free, and, in
addition, industrious youths are able to earn gratui-
ties, which have to be deposited in a savings bank
until their indentures are completed, on which they
are paid over in one sum. The theoretical instruction
comprises freehand, technical and conventional drawing, perspective, descriptive geometry, calculation,
and technology of wood, which together occupy some
thirty hours a week, and practical work occupies
about the same time.

CHAPTER XXIII

THE WOOD-CARVING INDUSTRY OF BRIENZ

ONE has only to look round the handsome little building known as the *Industriehalle*, or Hall of Industry, of Brienz, which rises in the centre of the village, in order to be assured that the wood-carving industry of this part of the Bernese Oberland owes much to nature and to natural characteristics. It would be strange were it otherwise. The exquisite situation and environment of Brienz — the scenes and incidents of Alpine life which the inhabitant witnesses every day, the wealth of suggestiveness in physical feature, in flora and fauna—could hardly fail to stimulate the artistic faculty and endow the brain and hand with a cunning and *finesse* which training alone could hardly have given. Yet it is only right to remember that two, and nearly three, generations of Brienzers have now been engaged in this industry, so that if there is anything in the theory of inherited aptitudes—a theory which, by the way, Herbert Spencer and August Weismann would more advantageously fight out on the floor of a Yorkshire factory than in their studies—the wood-carvers of Brienz ought to have a word to say on this phase of the great evolution question.

As in the case of some other house industries of Switzerland, wood-carving owed its origin to that necessity which has at all times been the parent of inventiveness. But the carving with which the Brienz turner, Christian Fischer, was wont to supplement his frugal earnings some eighty years ago was very primitive and unsophisticated—toys, knick-knacks, fancy articles somewhat flagrantly distinguished by paucity of fancy—compared with the works of true art which are now-a-days produced in many an unpretentious cottage on the shores of the blue lake which Turner painted with such marvellous power. But it was a beginning, small as it was, and in that way the foundations of the present flourishing industry were laid. Prosperity, however, came only late in the day. Long after the family of Christian Fischer ceased to have a monopoly of the craft—for other Brienzers were poor as well as he, and there was an agricultural problem even then—his simple models gave the cue to local talent. There was progressive improvement in execution, but little refinement in conception, and of art it was still premature to speak.

It was towards the end of the thirties that the first art school was formed, and that thus the first instruction in the theory of their handicraft was imparted to the carvers of Brienz. From that date wood-carving might count as an art-industry. The school had not long been in private hands before the Government of the canton appears to have suspected that Brienz had hit upon a good thing, and it wisely decided to help the industry on by the provision of skilled instructors. In time, however, the State began to weary in well-doing and private initiative had once more—in the form of the Association for Public Utility—to step in and make itself responsible for the proper training of the rising generation of carvers. The credit of having maintained the industry in a condition of efficiency down to the year 1884, when, as already explained, the system of technical instruction in Switzerland was entirely remodelled, belongs to this Association.

On its present basis the Wood-carving School of Brienz dates from that year, since when it has enjoyed the full benefit of the Federal subsidy offered to all technical and industrial institutions in the land. Young people can enter the school as apprentices directly they have "absolved" the nine years during which attendance at the elementary school is required by law, that is, at the age of fifteen, though pupils are indeed taken at any age up to thirty. The ordinary course of instruction is spread over three years, and any one remaining beyond that term does so voluntarily and by arrangement with the managers, who are nine in number, and are appointed equally by the canton, the communal council, and the members of the ecclesiastical parish of Brienz. It must be admitted that the pupils are very liberally dealt with. An entrance fee of ten francs (8s.) is imposed, but there are no fees and material is provided gratis, though security to the amount of fifty francs (£2) in the case of natives and 100 francs (£4) in the case of foreigners is required for the completion of the full term of apprenticeship. From the second year the pupil receives half the selling value of the work he does, and premiums are also offered to the exceptionally efficient and industrious from the beginning. On the half-proceeds system a young man of fair talent and application is able to earn as much as 800 francs (£32) in the course of the year, while the average for pupils of 16 to 19 years is about 500 francs (£20) yearly, which means much more on the Brienzersee than in an English town or even rural district.

Instruction is very thorough and systematic. The school is divided into two departments—the drawing and modelling school and the practical carving school —and there are three teachers: the head-master, who prepares designs and directs drawing generally, an instructor in carving, who has followed his art as a journeyman, and a modeller in clay and plaster of Paris. The school is carried on the whole year round with the exception of short holidays, and fifty-four hours are worked per week. The bulk of the time (thirty-six hours) naturally falls to carving in the workshop; then six each fall to modelling and free-hand drawing, and three each to designing and study of ornament. There are also separate evening draw-ing classes for adults and for boys. During a recent year there were nineteen apprentices in the carving school, all but two belonging to Brienz or the imme-diate neighbourhood, while in the two drawing schools forty young men and seventy-five boys were taught. The total number taught in connection with the school was 138, against 120 in the preceding year, a progress which of itself proves that the industry cannot be in an unhealthy state.

New pupils in carving are given pieces of lime wood to work upon, as it is both soft and cheap, and with the aid of drawings they practise simple orna-ment—geometrical figures in high relief and straight carving generally. After a youth has done this sort of work for a few weeks he can safely be set to simple curve and even leaf and flower carving. In time he begins to develop special tastes and aptitudes, and then he is encouraged to specialisation. This may take one of three directions. He may work at ornament (e.g. floral designs), at animal figures, or at the human figure. In the last event his ground-ing is very careful and minute. Beginning with the carving of individual parts of the body (eye, ear, mouth, finger, hand, foot, etc.), he gradually advances to more complex tasks—the face in relief, the head, or the whole body, as in the case of a crucifixion piece (a common study). As a rule an apprentice of ordinary capacity is able at the end of the first year to pass from the merely tuitional and experimental stage to practical work—working now with walnut, which is found in the locality—and indeed it is astonishing to see what beautiful carving is often done by quite young pupils.

At the end of the course the pupils either get work with employers, or work at home (forty francs will set a man up with bench and tools), or continue at the school on the half-proceeds system, the understanding being that the moiety of their earnings is paid to them whether the finished articles are sold or not.

The working apprentices are subject to ordinary school discipline. From morning to night, save for intervals for meals, the carving-rooms are a scene of quiet activity. There is no idle talking, no smoking, no frivolity of any kind, though the workers may not ever be under the taskmaster's eye. As to the kind of work done for sale, the head-master is left with a free hand. He is naturally guided by the demands of the market, and as taste changes rapidly his judgment and discretion are put to a severe test, though one which has hitherto been very successfully sustained. I notice that the last report of the Government Inspector gives the school this commendation :—" Organisation, curriculum, and the arrangements of the teachers are as good as ever. Excellent work is done and the teachers are always endeavouring to introduce originality both in the form and style of the articles carved."

It is remarkable how much is achieved by the Brienz Carving School with the aid of very modest resources. The sources of income are (1) sales of goods, which during a normal year amounted to 5673·65 francs (£227); (2) a federal subsidy of 2750 francs (£110); (3) a cantonal subsidy of 4346 francs (£174); (4) a contribution from the civil parish, 800 francs (£32); and (5) a contribution from the eccle- siastical parish, 700 francs (£28), giving a total of 16,024·67 francs, or £641. The expenditure during the same year was 14,978 francs, or nearly £600, from which the three teachers' salaries took the far too small share of 6200 francs (£248).

Since the beginning of 1894 the Brienz carving industry has had the help of a public Sample Exhi- bition. Under the auspices of the Association of the Oberland Woodwork Industry an *Industriehalle* has been opened here for the collection, display, and sale of the goods produced. Carved work can only be exhibited by members of the Association, who pay a small fee and also a commission on sales, and the articles they send must have been made by them- selves, in their works, or after their own designs. The exhibition, which, in spite of large sales, is always well stored with artistic and representative work, affords ample evidence of the skill and resource of the modern wood-carvers of the district, and probably few visitors to Brienz go away without inspecting and admiring it—none should do. There are chests and cupboards of wonderful design and surpassing delicacy of workmanship, unique over-mantels, chairs, picture-frames, animal groups, flower pieces,—indeed, almost everything of an ornamental kind that is made of wood, at any price between four francs and four hundred. At the time of my visit there was also on view one of the travelling collections of superb models which the Cantonal Museum at Berne sends periodically for the encouragement and emulation of the persevering Brienzers. The bulk of the association's trade is done with wholesale dealers in the large towns, yet the value of the goods sold to visitors is by no means inconsiderable. I was assured by one of the teachers that goods to the value of over half-a-million francs are sent away from Brienz yearly.

Before the industry was started the district was poor, and there was considerable emigration. To-day the emigration is small, and along the shores of the lake some 500 persons are steadily following a calling which affords a considerable return. Many of the carvers also carry on agriculture on a small scale. Now it is a small grazing farm, now a mere plot of land which only yields enough produce to cover the needs of the family. In these cases farming opera-

tions claim a large part of the summer months, and
the winter is devoted to carving. Yet from carving
alone earnings of 1000 and even 1500 francs in the
year are not uncommon, which may be regarded as
tolerable considering the modest demands made upon
life in this primitive part of the world. Existence
is simplicity itself; the houses are small and scantily
furnished; and farm produce and vegetables form
the staple food (meat is more or less a luxury), but
the people maintain a satisfied, if a toilsome and
contracted, existence.

Novel articles, showing originality of idea, sell
readiest, and a man with a speciality of his own may
count on having a good time of it. I was told of one
lucky carver who sent to the *Industriehalle* a group
of dogs upon which he placed the figure of 100
francs. It was snatched up at once, fresh commissions of the same sort flowed in plentifully, and ever
since then he has done nothing else. Nevertheless,
the complaint is made that the industry has suffered
owing to the intrusion of that bugbear of all handicraft, the irrepressible middleman, whose intercepted
gains have pressed prices down, but it is satisfactory
to know that the industry shows no clear signs of
decay.

VI

THE CONTROL OF THE DRINK TRAFFIC

CHAPTER XXIV

THE FEDERAL ALCOHOL MONOPOLY

TEN years have passed (1897) since the Government of the Confederation established a monopoly in the trade in alcohol. By the law of October 25, 1885, which came in force in 1887, the importation of alcohol, and the distillation of potatoes, cereals, and foreign fruit passed into the hands of the State. The distillation of home-grown fruit and the importation of foreign fruit-brandies (in consideration of a fee) were, however, allowed to remain free. Before this far-going project was legalised there were two appeals to the sense of the people upon the subject by the constitutional method of the *Referendum*— first upon the modification of the constitution which the measure would entail, and then upon the monopoly itself. Naturally those cantons and parts of cantons in which the large distilleries were situated furnished the principal opposition to the monopoly, while the wine-growing districts went solidly for it; but the scheme both times came through victorious by a substantial majority of votes.[1]

The only concession granted by the Alcohol Monopoly Law to private industry is that at least one-fourth of the home consumption of spirits must be made for the *Régie* by private concerns existing by State concession; while the rest may or may not be imported by the *Régie* at will. In accepting tenders for the fourth part of the supply, however, distilleries worked on a co-operative basis are supposed to have the preference, and the amounts allotted to single concerns vary from 150 to 1000 hectolitres. The condition is also imposed that only such a price shall be paid as covers the actual cost of producing the brandy, without reckoning the residuary liquors, the value of the latter being, in other words, the profit which the distiller may reap on the transaction. The *Régie* only supplies spirit and drinking-brandy in quantities of at least 125 kilogr. or 150 litres, so that its transactions are of a wholesale character, the small retail business being left entirely to private persons. As to the further dealing with brandy, it is provided by the law that the sale of brandy of all kinds in quantities of not less than 40 litres is a

---

[1] It may be explained that when any modification of the constitution is voted upon, there is necessary to its success a double majority—a majority of the cantons and a majority of the aggregate voters. In other cases a majority of votes alone is sufficient.

free trade. The sale of smaller quantities for consumption may take place on or off the premises, but in either case subject to taxation and regulation by the cantonal authorities. Where the spirit is used for technical purposes it is sold at cost price (*plus* the duty if imported); where for drinking an excess sum (called *Monopolzuschlag*) is added. Naturally the officials of the *Régie* reserve and, where necessary, exercise the right to control the manufacture of the spirit at every turn. The manufactured spirit is bonded in six depôts, three only of which belong to and are staffed by the *Régie*, while the others are rented.

It will be noticed that the State does not pretend to follow the alcohol after it has left its hands. It guarantees the sale of a pure product; but restrictions upon the after preparation of the spirit and provisions against adulteration are matters for the several cantons, so that the public is, so far as the Federal Government is concerned, offered no absolute surety. It will be seen later how this lack has been supplied in the canton of Basle Urban.

In the fixing of compensation to the expropriated distillers, account was alone taken of the depreciation which had been sustained by buildings, machinery, and appliances, owing to their being no longer used for distillation, and not at all of goodwill and forfeited business profits. Yet, though the law was very explicit on this point, it was contested

by some of the distillers, but, of course, unsuccess-
fully. Thus it came about that the amount of compensation which had eventually to be paid by the
State was ridiculously small compared with the enormous number of concerns, large and small, which
were supplanted. The number of claims was 1376.
Of these some 1200 were sustained, and the total
amount paid was 3,714,251 francs, or £148,570, an
average of about £124.

The objects in view in introducing the monopoly
were various :—(1) From the fiscal standpoint it was
desired to replace the old cantonal taxation, which
was neither uniform nor equal, by a form of taxation
which would bear lightly on the country in general.
(2) From the economic standpoint it was hoped to
promote the interests of agriculture. (3) From the
moral it was hoped to supply a better quality of
brandy, and yet to diminish the consumption of it.

To deal briefly with each of these phases of the
question :—

(1) Before the passing of the Alcohol Monopoly
Law no Federal tax was imposed on the manufacture
and sale of spirit, though there were import duties.
There existed in sixteen of the cantons, however, an
excise-tax which went by the name of *Ohmgeld*, and
this tax in process of time had in most cases been
converted into a sort of import duty. The cantons
chiefly affected by the monopoly were Berne, Lucerne,
Basle, Soleure, Freiburg, and Aargau, which had also

by far the largest consumption of alcohol, and suffered most from the brandy plague. All these cantons protected their distillery industry by duties on imported spirits, both home and foreign, and in order to insure a better sale for their own brandy, subjected wine and beer, of which they produced little, to heavy taxation. The old *Ohmgelder* and *octrois* were not only anomalous, but unjust, and a law of 1874 decreed their extinction (to date from 1890) without compensation. The financial loss to the cantons was, however, serious, for the proceeds of their particularist taxes had been about 3,580,880 francs, or £143,235; and, in order to make up for this, it was agreed that the total profits of the monopoly should be divided amongst the cantons. This surplus, however, was to be divided not according to the consumption of brandy—which would have been to place a premium on heavy drinking—but according to population. Furthermore, it was stipulated that one-tenth of each canton's share should be employed in combating intemperance (*Alcoholismus*). With the abolition of the *Ohmgelder* went hand-in-hand the repeal of the excise taxes on beer and brandy production, and, to a large extent, the tax on the retail sale of wine and beer (that is, on quantities under two litres), though the regulation of public-houses was left entirely in the hands of the cantons, and the result has been a general increase in the fees levied upon them. The general effect of all these measures has been to increase the price of liquors —brandy, wine, and beer—consumed in drinking-houses, and to cheapen those purchased in the open trade.

An enormous economy has also been effected for the country as a whole by replacing the former cumbersome and costly cantonal systems of *octrois* by a single federal *Régie*. The total cost of the alcohol administration (officials, rectifying house, depôts, etc.) has averaged £15,000 yearly, which is but a fraction of the cost of levying the old import duties in the cantons, while the proceeds of the latter were barely more than half the proceeds of the monopoly.

(2) On the economic and commercial side the institution of the monopoly has been productive of important consequences, for it has revolutionised a great industry. "The Swiss distilleries" (I quote from M. Milliet, the Director of the Monopoly) "may be divided into two great categories. The first comprises the distillation of fruit, fruit refuse, wild berries, roots, etc.; the second the distillation of all other stuffs, and especially cereals. The fruit distilleries are only affected in so far as they use foreign raw material, and the reason for this is that fruit distillation is one of the most important of rural industries in Switzerland—an industry which provides modest gains to innumerable small farmers—and any interference with these would have been a serious matter." As to fruit distillation, M. Milliet contends

that it has not only maintained its old position, but has experienced further development, inasmuch as the country has become independent of foreign producers for the additional quantity which is now consumed. The distillation of starch-containing substances, on the other hand, whose continuation appeared only possible in the form of large concerns, has been maintained in an efficient state in concerns of moderate size.

It is regarded as a merit of the scheme—and certainly it is one of its consequences—that the monopoly has abolished both the smallest and the largest distilleries. It is held by the friends of the monopoly that neither truly served the interests of agriculture or of the public. The small distilleries produced a liquor of inferior quality, while their output was inconsiderable. Against these concerns, too, much unfavourable evidence of a moral kind had accumulated. A report of the Federal Department for Home Affairs issued in 1886 stated :—

" In many cases the small distilleries, in consequence of their structural connection with the dwellings and their facility of access, and of the direct participation of members of the family therein, have become seats of contagion, so that the indulgence in brandy has seized upon one member after another, the habit of indulgence has been conveyed to neighbours, and often enough has infected the entire neighbourhood." Not only so, but from these concerns

more than from the large proceeded a noxious system
of retailing from house to house on terms so easy
and so tempting that an excessive consumption of
brandy was encouraged amongst poor people. That
this was not an imaginary evil is proved by the fact
that in the canton of Berne some hundreds of small
distilleries had long before 1885 been abolished by
law. Only the Confederate States acting together,
however, could apply a radical remedy for what was
a notorious social disease.

On the other hand, the large distilleries imported
the greater part of their raw stuffs, preferring cheap
maize from abroad to home-grown cereals and potatoes, and this was a standing grievance with the
farmers of the North and East. At any rate they
all disappeared. "This is a democracy!" said M.
Milliet to me in conversation upon the subject. "We
have eliminated the great capitalists—for that is
what it amounted to—and it was a good thing for
the country. The big distilleries bought all their
raw products abroad, and so they were of no benefit
to home agriculture." Hence it has come about
that, in place of some 1450 private distilleries of all
kinds and sizes, there are now some 63 distilleries
of moderate size working for the State, and to that
end fully equipped with modern appliances. These
are unable without permission to employ any other
than home-grown raw material, and for their spirit
they receive a price which allows of their paying the

farmers remunerative prices for their products. They are also said to be well pleased with the new arrangement, for they have a sure and adequate income—working, indeed, on commission with guaranteed full occupation, and virtually no trade risks.

(3) As to the moral side of the question, there is no denying that the monopoly has exercised a beneficial influence. It would be wrong to say, as has frequently been said, that the prime motive of the monopoly was to promote temperance, though this purpose was 'one among others, and has in some degree been attained.

"The action of the State," M. Milliet has said, " is directed towards the substitution of the intemperate indulgence in brandy by a temperate use of wine and beer. Those who condemn the drinking of alcohol in every form will not, of course, regard so circumscribed a programme as an ideal. Yet even the abstainer will allow that there is relative advantage in a diminution of the use of that alcoholic beverage whose effect is most brutalising, and the Swiss abstainer in particular must allow that only utter doctrinaireism can regard the achievement of that end as unimportant in a country in which abstainers form an insignificant minority of the people."

Whether the somewhat higher price of brandy be the reason, or some other circumstance, it is a fact that the consumption of the spirit has materially decreased since the monopoly came into force. In 1882, five years before the monopoly began, the average consumption per head of the population was 9·40 litres; in 1885, the year of the law being passed, it was 10·26 litres; in 1890, after it had been in operation three years (from 1887) it was 6·27 litres; in 1891, 6·32; and in 1894, 6·0 litres. Even allowing for the uncertainty of statistics—and these are M. Milliet's—a reduction of 25 per cent. seems a moderate and safe figure. On the other hand, it is stated that the consumption of wine has increased from 55 or 60 litres per head in 1885 to from 75 to 80 litres, and that of beer from 36 litres to 50 litres in the interval. If this displacement has really taken place, as the friends of the monopoly claim, it must be admitted to be a relative advantage and a commendation of the State's action when one compares the physical and moral effects of the use of spirits on the one hand and the light wine and beer common in Switzerland on the other hand.[1] As before, the chief consumers of brandy are to be found in the cantons of Berne, Soleure, Freiburg, Basle, and Geneva.

[1] The report for 1895 of the Commission de l'Hospice Général of Geneva (which discharges the poor-law functions of that city) states : "The population has not unhappily the reputation of being sober and provident ; the indulgence in wine is small in comparison with that in alcohol in its various forms. This last is a poison which kills slowly, depriving its devotees of all energy, all faculty of working, and of health."

There has been a certain amount of irregularity in the application of the "tenth" part of the profits of the monopoly (familiarly known as *das Alcoholzehntel*), which should legally go to the combating of intemperance. No doubt the words allow a wide latitude of interpretation; at any rate, they have been loosely read by most, if not all, the cantonal authorities. Among the purposes to which the "tenth" has been applied are the establishment and maintenance of houses for inebriates, reformatories, asylums for imbeciles, the blind, and the deaf and dumb, orphanages, and hospitals; contributions to technical schools, herberges and other workmen's houses of call, holiday colonies, public libraries, people's coffee-houses, soup kitchens, total abstinence and good templar societies, and other temperance organisations; agencies for feeding poor scholars, and sending the weaklings of the towns into the country, and in miscellaneous poor relief. The "tenth" amounts to a substantial sum, the average for the five years, 1890 to 1894, being 571,412 francs, or £22,856, while the amount in 1894 was 450,955 francs, or £18,038. The average shares in the proceeds of the monopoly which fell to the various cantons during the 8½ years of its existence, 1887 to 1895, were as given in the table on the following page.

Canton.	Total share in 8½ years. Francs.	Per head of the population (1888) yearly. Francs.
Geneva	3,236,453. 62	3·64
Uri	457,340. 44	3·17
Freiburg	2,639,767. 28	2·65
Soleure	1,846,615. 31	2·58
Lucerne	2,880,457. 49	2·54
Berne	8,767,351. 06	1·95
Grisons	1,328,099. 29	1·66
Ticino	1,743,755. 06	1·65
Vaud	3,424,108. 26	1·63
Glarus	455,460. 19	1·62
Nidwalden	163,831. 56	1·57
Obwalden	192,899. 29	1·54
Aargau	2,481,236. 12	1·54
Basle (Land)	774,638. 74	1·49
Zug	280,964. 94	1·46
Basle (Town)	885,753. 30	1·43
Valais	1,186,693. 17	1·40
Zurich	3,764,837. 21	1·33
Schwyz	559,391. 37	1·33
Schaffhausen	420,570. 58	1·33
Appenzell, a.R.	601,741. 54	1·33
„ i.R.	143,284. 50	1·33
St. Gall	2,546,863. 74	1·33
Thurgau	1,167,251. —	1·33
Neuchâtel	1,210,733. 80	1·33
Total	43,160,098. 86	1·64

In the serious vested interest which every canton thus has in the monopoly, lies, perhaps, the greatest guarantee of the permanence of the institution, though it would probably survive on its own merits even were self-interest no factor in the case. I quote some words of M. Milliet, as embodying a sober estimate of the results so far achieved :—

" The revision of the constitution in 1885, and the laws which proceeded therefrom, deserve neither the unrestrained praise of enthusiasts nor the nagging criticism of those who always ' know better.' They furnish no flawless and perfect solution of a socio-political problem, but, like the decree regarding the curtailment of the hours of labour and our legislation on popular rights, they are important stages on the way to the solution of the questions which lie before the legislators of the twentieth century."

CHAPTER XXV

THE MUNICIPAL ALCOHOL MONOPOLY AT BASLE

THE proposal which is popular with a certain school of English temperance reformers, that towns should be given the option of taking over the management of the drink traffic, suggests an appeal to the experience of the municipality of Basle. The restrictive monopoly which exists there applies, however, to alcohol only. In all probability it was suggested to the authorities by the Federal alcohol monopoly legalised in 1885, and operative from the year 1887, and Basle could the more easily adopt it since the town forms of itself a semi-canton with independent jurisdiction and (within fixed competence) independent legislature. By a law of April, 1888, the Cantonal Government took over the retail trade in pure spirit in quantities of less than 40 litres, and of brandy of every quality prepared by admixture of spirit with water, essences, extracts, or roots, as regards quantities of less than 40 litres, whether draught or bottled. Liqueurs are exempt, though these are only allowed to be sold in closed, sealed, and capsuled bottles, and then subject to a licence and to police sanction. The spirit is supplied to the retailers in the qualities supplied by the Federal Alcohol Administration, and it may be purchased from no other source. The preparation of the spirit in the forms required for public consumption is left with the retailers, though the Cantonal Government exercises control here likewise.

The monopoly, as in the case of the Federal monopoly, was not established as a fiscal expedient, and as a matter of fact the Cantonal Government derives but a small surplus after the necessary costs of the control and general administration have been defrayed, though the opportunity of enriching itself is virtually unlimited. While thus the canton cannot be said to profit financially by the institution, the profits of the retailers are strictly limited, for their average earnings are fixed at 15 centimes (about 1½d.) per litre.

The sellers are required to expose the official price list to the view of their customers, and the prices therein stated may not be exceeded. It may be interesting to give the rates now ruling, with the profits allowed to the retailers:

	Price per litre Francs	Profit Centimes
Superior Spirit	1.80	23
Marc (*Trester*)	0.90	15
Lees (*Drusen*)	1.0	15
Cumin Brandy (*Kümmel*)	1.0	15
Bilberry ,, (*Heidelbeer*)	1.0	20
Aniseed (*Aenis*)	1.0	15
Nut Brandy (*Nusswasser*)	1.0	20
Peppermint (*Pfeffermünz*)	1.20	20

The retail sale of spirit is permitted in twenty-five places, a number far less than before the monopoly came into force. These places are licensed by the municipality and are located as equally throughout the towns as possible. No fee is charged, though each licencee is required to give surety for legality and good behaviour to the amount of 500 francs (£20). The licences are given indefinitely as to time, being virtually *ad vitam aut culpam*, though this is neither stated nor allowed to be understood. In strict form the Government reserves full right to cancel or withdraw a licence at will, and that without compensation of any kind. In case of the removal or death of a licencee, his successor in business has no claim to a continuance of the concession, and there cannot be such a thing as the sale of the privilege from one to another, because of the uncertainty and the risk of discovery. The mode of procedure in such cases is for the Government to declare the licence vacant and to invite suitable applications. All these are considered on their merits, importance being attached to the character of the applicant, and the eligibility of his premises, and it may or may not happen that the licence is allowed to attach further to the same premises.

For the monopoly it is claimed with justification that it has improved the quality of the spirit offered for consumption. Here the Federal monopoly falls short. Applying only to raw spirit, it offers no guarantee of the quality of the products of alcohol which ultimately find their way into the market. The drastic regulation of the retail trade which exists in Basle does, however, afford this guarantee, and no one denies that in practice it is a success. Not only so, but the monopoly has gradually led to a diminution of consumption. The amount of alcohol retailed in various forms is less absolutely as well as relatively to population than before the monopoly was established. This will be seen from the following official figures :

			Increase.	Decrease.
1889	123,458 litres			
1890	137,194 „	...	13,736 litres	
1891	131,811 „	...		5,383 litres
1892	129,457 „	...		2,354 „
1893	117,087 „	...		12,370 „
1894	110,346 „	...		6,741 „
1895	107,633 „	...		2,713 „

As compared with 1889 the decrease in 1895 was 15,825 litres or 12·8 per cent., though the population had in the meantime increased from 74,245 (1888) to over 82,000. On the contrary, the consumption of wine and bottled beer has considerably increased, which the authorities regard as a clear gain from the moral standpoint.

CHAPTER XXVI

THE LICENSING LAWS OF CANTONS BASLE AND ZURICH

THE federalising of the wholesale trade in brandy led some of the cantons to revise their general licensing arrangements, and Basle and Zurich may be taken as typical instances. The licensing law (*Wirthschafts-Gesetz*) of Canton Basle Urban, which is dated December 19, 1887, and has been in operation since April 1, 1888, contains some very noteworthy features. It divides licences into three kinds—(1) those for ordinary inns, lodging guests; (2) those for wine and beer houses of the restaurant species, and for clubs; and (3) occasional licences. The retail trade in alcoholic liquors also falls into three classes —(1) the sale of wine and beer; (2) the sale of spirits; and (3) the sale of wine and beer by employers to their workpeople. Variable fees are attached to the foregoing licences, and in the city these fees go to the exchequer of the canton, while in the rural parishes half the fees go to the cantonal exchequer and half to the parish in which the licences are granted. There can be no transfer of

294

a licence from one person or place to another without permission.

The only singular licence is the "factory licence," by virtue of which an employer may sell liquor to his workpeople during the ordinary work-pauses. This provision led in the summer of 1895 to a formal protest on the part of the masons of the city, who petitioned for its abolition, on the ground that in their case, at least, the foremen under whom they worked forced drink upon them.

It is required that the holder of a liquor licence shall himself reside on the licensed premises, though in exceptional cases a deputy, if possessed of all the specified qualifications, may be permitted by the police.

Inns and other drinking-houses are divided into twelve classes according as they pay annual licence fees of £8, £12, £16, £20, £24, £32, £40, £48, £56, £64, £72, or £80, though in rural parishes the fee may be reduced to as little as £6. Refreshment-houses, however, which do not supply spirituous liquors, pay from £2 to £12, and if their purpose is benevolent they may be freed altogether, while occasional licences cost from 4s. to 16s. in the case of persons already licensed, and as much as £20 in other cases. The licence to sell wine and beer by retail and the factory licence vary from £2 to £12, while the licence to sell spirit varies from £1 4s. to £20 according to circumstances.

Inns and drinking-places are subject to special restrictions. Vagrants, beggars, and bad characters may not be systematically served with liquor, nor may children of school-going age at any time, while "young persons under eighteen years of age" may not be afforded "the opportunity of excessive drinking or of gambling." The over-working of attendants is expressly prohibited, and at least seven hours of unbroken rest must be ensured at night, with one free afternoon a week for recreation; while girls under eighteen years of age who do not belong to the licencee's family may not be employed in public service. After ten o'clock at night "no noisy talk" may be indulged in, though there may be "respectable singing" for an hour later, and in summer music may be permitted until the same hour if the neighbours do not object. This, however, like dancing, is dependent upon police sanction.

The licensing arrangements of the canton of Zurich were placed under new regulations in 1896. The law on the subject was submitted to the customary *Referendum* on May 31, 1896, when 42,238 votes were given in favour and 15,601 against, and it came into operation on July 1 following. This law requires every person who keeps a lodging-house, who sells food and drinks to be consumed on the premises, or who sells spirituous liquors by retail, to take out a State (cantonal) licence (*Patent*).

Licensed houses are of the following kinds—(1)

hotels and inns, entitled to lodge guests, and to supply food and drinks to be consumed on or off the premises; (2) refreshment-houses, entitled to sell food and drinks for consumption on or off the premises; (3) *hôtels garnis*, entitled to lodge guests; (4) coffee, temperance, and similar refreshment houses, where alcoholic drinks are not sold; (5) confectioners' shops under a like restriction; and (6) private boarding-houses (*pensions*) with more than five boarders where they supply alcoholic drinks to the latter at other times than at meal-times.

It is stipulated that a licence attaches to the holder personally and is granted for a year at a time, with no claim whatever to prolongation. It is competent for a licencee, however, to transfer the licence from one place to another in the same parish, but there can be no transference from one parish to another without a fresh licence being sought. In either case new licence-fees are payable. Licences, moreover, are only granted to thoroughly capable persons of good reputation, who have been resident in the canton for at least a year, though the latter condition can be waived in special cases.

No person who has been punished for an offence against morality can at any time hold a licence, and a person convicted of any other common offences becomes disqualified for a period of ten years, while temporary deprivation of civil rights entails concurrent disqualification. If the licence of a house has been repeatedly taken away on account of offences against the public law the same premises cannot be licensed again for a period of two years. Moreover, should a licencee become incapable of managing his business or lose his civil rights, he forfeits his licence at once without claim to compensation. At any time during the year a licence can be annulled without compensation in the event of a breach of the law or of the licencee proving not to possess all the requisite qualifications. If it be expedient to continue a licence surrendered under such circumstances it must be offered for competition, and the recipient must be decided by casting lots. A licence can only be transferred to another person when the licencee dies and his heirs wish to succeed him, and when he becomes bankrupt and the trustees of the estate deem it expedient to continue the business.

Special conditions apply to hotels and inns and general refreshment-houses where alcoholic liquors are sold. Many persons are disqualified from engaging in such businesses, among them members of the Cantonal Government and the Supreme Court, Government Solicitors, and other judicial functionaries, various administrative officials, the clergy, teachers, and notaries, while the parishes individually are also empowered at will to exclude justices of the peace and civil officials.

Permission to open new licensed houses must in general be refused when the number of such houses already exceeds the requirements of the parish or locality respectively, and can be held to be injurious to the public welfare. This is deemed to be the case when in the parish or quarter of the parish concerned there is a licensed house to less than 200 inhabitants, though this condition is not to apply in exceptional cases, as for example in rural parishes covering a wide area, in new quarters, in busy trading localities, and in the precincts of railway stations.

Stringent regulations are laid down for the internal management of drinking-houses, especially in the interest of their employees. It is required that the children of the house shall as far as possible be kept out of the public rooms. Girls under twenty years not belonging to the landlord's family and youths under sixteen years may not be employed regularly in serving guests. All employees must be secured at least eight hours of uninterrupted rest between the hours of eight p.m. and eight a.m., and they must not be employed for any purpose whatever after midnight, though exceptions are allowed on the occasion of festivals, balls, and private gatherings. It is permissible to employ servants under sixteen years for domestic purposes, but not to an extent that may injure their health, and a maximum service of eight hours daily is laid down, with nine p.m. as the latest hour. Every week each employee must be given an uninterrupted rest of at least six hours between the hours of eight a.m. and eight p.m., and every three weeks a full free day, though this latter may be exchanged for two holidays a year of at least four days at once. Any infraction of these provisions may be punished by a fine of from 8s. to £12. All houses must be closed (except to travellers) on the forenoons of festivals until eleven o'clock, and the parishes have the option of applying this restriction to Sundays likewise, while they may also fix a closing hour for the evenings generally. The supplying of drink to inebriates, as also to youths under sixteen years of age, unless accompanied by adults or travelling through, is forbidden under penalty. There are special regulations for the dancing which plays such an important part in the recreative life of rural districts. On six Sundays in the year public dancing may take place in the licensed houses without special sanction. These days are fixed by the local authorities, which, however, must give preference to certain of the local festivals. Dancing can only be held at other times—whether Sundays or week-days—by permission, and then subject to conditions.

The cost of the licence for a hotel or inn is proportionate to its patronage, and twenty different fees, rising from £4 to £80, are fixed by the law, though in rural parishes the cost may be as low as £2. The licences for *hôtels garnis*, confectioners' shops, and boarding-houses vary from £2 to £20; those for coffee, temperance, and similar houses from £2 to £8; while the cost of an off-licence is as follows :—

For the sale of wine, beer, and must, 16s. to £8; for wine, beer, must, and spirits, £1 4s. to £12; and for spirits alone, 8s. to £16. All the proceeds of the licences go in the first place to the State, but it returns twenty-five per cent. of the gross amount to the parishes, this being divided throughout the canton according to population at the end of every year.

APPENDIX

I.—VARIANT NAMES OF THE SWISS CANTONS

GERMAN.	FRENCH.
Zürich.	Zurich.
Bern.	Berne.
Luzern.	Lucerne.
Uri.	Uri.
Schwyz.	Schwyz.
Unterwalden { Obwalden, Nidwalden.	Unterwald { Unterwald - le - Haut, Unterwald - le - Bas.
Glarus.	Glaris.
Zug.	Zoug.
Freiburg.	Fribourg.
Solothurn.	Soleure.
{ Basel-Stadt, Baselland.	{ Bâle-Ville, Bâle-Campagne.
Schaffhausen.	Schaffhouse.
{ Appenzell, ausser-Rhoden. Appenzell, inner-Rhoden.	{ Appenzell, Rhod.-ext. Appenzell, Rhod.-int.
Graubünden.	Grisons.
St. Gallen.	St. Gall.
Aargau.	Argovie.
Thurgau.	Thurgovie.
Tessin.	Tessin (Italian—Ticino).
Waadt.	Vaud.
Wallis.	Valais.
Neuenburg.	Neuchâtel.
Genf.	Genève.

II.—THE SWISS CURRENCY

In the foregoing pages it has occasionally been inconvenient, in dealing with small sums, to state the exact equivalent in English money. For the sake of reference a table of equations is given :—

		s.	d.				s.	d.
5 centimes	=		0½	12 francs	=		9	7
10 ,,	=		1	13 ,,	=		10	4½
50 ,,	=		4¾	14 ,,	=		11	2½
1 franc	=		9½	15 ,,	=		12	0
2 francs	=	1	7	16 ,,	=		12	9½
3 ,,	=	2	4½	17 ,,	=		13	7
4 ,,	=	3	2½	18 ,,	=		14	5
5 ,,	=	4	0	19 ,,	=		15	2½
6 ,,	=	4	9½	20 ,,	=		16	0
7 ,,	=	5	7	21 ,,	=		16	9½
8 ,,	=	6	5	22 ,,	=		17	7½
9 ,,	=	7	2½	23 ,,	=		18	5
10 ,,	=	8	0	24 ,,	=		19	2½
11 ,,	=	8	9½	25 ,,	=		20	0

THE END

Richard Clay & Sons, Limited, London & Bungay.

In two volumes, demy 8vo.   Price 26s.

GERMANY AND THE GERMANS

Social Life, Culture, Religious Life, Politics and Parties, Socialism, and the Makers of Germany.

SOME OPINIONS OF THE PRESS.

The Saturday Review :—"Mr. Dawson's previous writings on German affairs have accustomed us to look for good work at his hands; and in his 'Germany and the Germans' we are not disappointed, though it is impossible to give the book unmixed approval.   But having had our grumble, we may turn to the more agreeable business of giving hearty praise to the bulk of the work, of which much is really valuable, and nearly all interesting. . . . Mr. Dawson's chapters on education are so good that we wish he had treated some parts of the subject in even greater detail. . . . The chapters on political parties deserve to have many readers."

The Athenæum :—"There was room for this book . . . . displays both knowledge and judgment.   The author is seen at his best in his lively and sympathetic sketches of the social life of Germany.   Nothing could be better in its way than his account of the effects produced by military discipline on the mass of the population, and no one has shown more conclusively how many good reasons there are for the general popularity of the German army."

ᴸ *The Times :*—"Full of actuality. . . . The note of the book is keen observation, combined with a certain self-confidence which, however sustained by wide knowledge and painstaking study, is a little dogmatic at times."

The Standard :—"There is much shrewd observation and detailed knowledge, as well as abundant common-sense, in these two volumes. . . . His work is a study of institutions and manners—the outcome of personal impressions, informed throughout by judgment, and the constant and painstaking attempt to get at actual facts. . . . Mr. Dawson has quite evidently attempted to look with frank and impartial eyes at every aspect of German society, and though he is a candid and outspoken critic, he certainly cannot be accused —with, perhaps, the majority of Englishmen—of insular prejudice."

The Daily Telegraph :—(For some years) "no information respecting the youngest of modern Empires has reached the British reading public equalling in authenticity, interest, and instructiveness that contained in the two handsome volumes now given to publicity by Mr. W. H. Dawson, under the title of 'Germany and the Germans.'—This excellent work—a literary monument of intelligent and conscientious labour—deals with every phase and aspect of State and political activity," etc.

The Daily Chronicle :—"With Mr. Dawson's two volumes before him, the ordinary reader may well afford to dispense with the perusal of previous authorities on Germany. Books like dynasties can be deposed, and in the 'battle of books' which is likely to result from the appearance of Mr. Dawson's octavo tomes, it seems probable enough that he will be able to hold the field. . . . He possesses this quality of the best writers, that he never seems to allow his own particular English sympathies to colour his estimates of men and things in Germany."

Westminster Gazette :—"A perusal of Mr. Dawson's book leaves a decidedly favourable impression. . . . The book, which is brightly written throughout, must be regarded as a valuable addition to the average Englishman's knowledge of Germany and its people."

The Speaker :—"A work like this, dealing with the leading aspects of the national life (of Germany) in a really broad and scientific spirit, ought to command attention."

St. James's Gazette :—"The author criticizes many German ideas and institutions, but he does so without arrogance and bitterness, and about characteristics which command his sympathy he writes with cordial appreciation, sometimes even with enthusiasm."

The Globe :—"The book can be heartily recommended as being both informing and readable. . . . One is struck at once by its unpretentiousness and thoroughness. . . . Throughout, Mr. Dawson's outlook is clear and fair."

The Spectator :—"Those who wish to enlarge their information on the social and religious life, culture, politics and parties of Germany, may consult the present book with advantage.   Mr. Dawson writes well and from experience, and has few prejudices."

The National Observer :—"The work displays thought and keen perception, accurate observation, good sense, and its information is set forth well enough."

The Morning Post :—"By close observation, combined with a faculty for recording his impressions in an impartial and forcible style, Mr. W. H. Dawson, in his studies of German life, has produced a work of considerable value."

LONDON : CHAPMAN AND HALL, Lᴅ.

www.ingramcontent.com/pod-product-compliance
Lightning Source LLC
Chambersburg PA
CBHW031358270326
41929CB00010BA/1233